Lives of the Prophets

Retold and illustrated by
Elma Ruth Harder

with a foreword by
Zafar Ishaq Ansari

For you, Tahira,
and your lovely family.

Salam,
Elma
June 20, 1999

OXFORD
UNIVERSITY PRESS

OXFORD
UNIVERSITY PRESS

Great Clarendon Street, Oxford OX2 6DP

Oxford University Press is a department of the University of Oxford.
It furthers the University's objective of excellence in research, scholarship,
and education by publishing worldwide in

Oxford New York

Athens Auckland Bangkok Bogotá Buenos Aires Calcutta
Cape Town Chennai Dar es Salaam Delhi Florence Hong Kong Istanbul
Karachi Kuala Lumpur Madrid Melbourne Mexico City Mumbai
Nairobi Paris São Paulo Singapore Taipei Tokyo Toronto Warsaw

with associated companies in Berlin Ibadan

Oxford is a registered trade mark of Oxford University Press
in the UK and in certain other countries

First published 1999

ISBN 0 19 579043 X

Printed in Pakistan at
Asian Packages, Karachi.
Published by
Ameena Saiyid, Oxford University Press
5-Bangalore Town, Sharae Faisal
PO Box 13033, Karachi-75350, Pakistan.

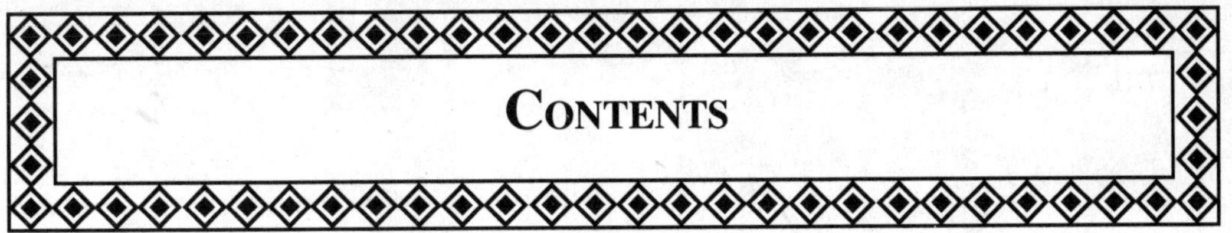

Contents

For Noor and Basit

FOREWORD

Written by a Canadian Muslim, the stories depicting the lives of the Prophets have been retold in this book with two characteristic features: they are based on the Glorious Qur'an with scarcely any embellishment, and they have been written for the young readers with special attention to a style and vocabulary that would conform to their level of comprehension and linguistic competence.

The book falls in the well-established genre of *Qasas al-Anbiya'* (Stories of the Prophets) which developed quite early in Islamic history. Muslims believe that all Prophets have essentially brought the same message from the same source. Throughout history, God has sent His Messengers to guide humanity and the Prophet Muhammad (May the Peace and Blessings of Allah be upon him) brought the final message for all human beings. This belief has given birth to a worldview in which all Prophets are looked upon as bearers of Divine Message, and in conformity with the teachings of the Qur'an, Muslims do not differentiate between one Prophet and the other.

With its captivating stories and instructive language, the *Lives of the Prophets* is bound to initiate a process of inquiry in the minds of its young readers. The most basic lesson they would learn from the book is the essential unity of the message which the Prophets brought for humanity. They would find out that the message sent by God to all human beings has certain basic elements which have remained unchanged over the course of centuries and millennia. They would also realize that God's guidance is not restricted to a particular region or people, and that all Prophets instructed their people to follow the same guidance. This universality of Islam's worldview is particularly important in a world drawing closer through rapid means of communication. Let us hope that an enhanced awareness of this will not only bring God's creatures closer to God, but also closer to each other.

Lives of the Prophets also brings forth the travails and struggles of many Prophets who faced opposition to their mission from their nations. The broad sweep of the book takes the readers to the ancient cities, deserts, mountains and landscapes full of captivating grandeur. Through these stories, children would find inspiration to develop their lives on the pattern of the highest models set forth by the best specimens of humanity. The moral and spiritual guidance persistently present in the lives of the Prophets would become model for their behaviour as they learn the virtues of honesty, truthful behaviour and sincere devotion to God.

The strongest characteristic of these stories is faith in God. It is through this faith that human beings were able to endure tremendous hardships and difficulties. Consider the examples of Yaqoob (Jacob) who wept for his lost child but who kept his faith intact and whose prayers were ultimately answered. Or the tremendous difficulties faced by Musa (Moses) in his attempts to guide his people to God who had taken humans as their gods. These detailed accounts inspire one to be persistent and patient in one's faith.

Another important feature of these stories is their cumulative impact. The stories of the Prophets have an internal symmetry, harmony and commonality. The book brings this out very clearly. The denial of the various Prophets by their community, the patient preaching of the message by the Prophets and the eventual result of obstinately rejecting that message—all these are presented in the book with graphic details. The combined impact of this persistent pattern instills awe of God and a liking for righteous behaviour. The moral bearing of the book is particularly important for the formative years of one's life.

Above all, these stories have an irresistible appeal as models of excellent human behaviour. From the dramatic incidents in the life of Musa to the details of captivity and release of Yusuf (Joseph), the stories present a wonderful panorama of events—all skillfully told in a language which children can understand.

Apart from its other merits, the book—written, as it is, by a Canadian Muslim—is one of the several manifestations of a change that is coming about in the cultural life of the *ummah* of Islam. For a long, long time the Muslims of Europe and America were mainly on the receiving end of the Islamic discourse. Notwithstanding some honourable exceptions such as that of Muhammad Asad, the contributions that the Western Muslims made to that discourse were not numerous, and were scarcely of any significant impact. One big change that was noted in the seventies of the present century was the presence of three Muslim intellectual stalwarts—Fazlur Rahman, Ismail al-Faruqi, and Seyyed Hossein Nasr—in USA.

They were, however, émigré. Each of them had moved to the new world from a major centre of Islamic thought and culture—South Asia, the Arab world and Iran. We have, however, been witnessing in recent years a steady stream of native Western Muslim intellectuals—Roger Garaudy, Murad Hofmann, Jeffery Lang, Michael Wolf, Gai Eaton, Alija Izetbegovic—to mention just a few of them, who are contributing to the contemporary Islamic discourse.

These contributions are bound to have an impact on the religious outlook of Muslims all over the world, including those in the heartlands of Islam. This should be greeted as a salutary development that befits the universal character of Islam and betokens for it a great promise.

Oxford University Press deserves to be wholeheartedly complimented for publishing this enlightening and readable book.

Islamabad
November 1998

Zafar Ishaq Ansari
Director General
Islamic Research Institute
International Islamic University

Assalamo Alaikum, young readers!

In this book you will find stories from the Noble Qur'an about the prophets. These persons were specially chosen by Allah to guide humanity. You will read about their problems and the ways they had to struggle against non-believers and unjust rulers. You will discover how they had a strong understanding of what was right and what was wrong. You will see that their faith in Allah was unfailing. They were heroes.

These stories have been retold here for you so that you can get a clear picture of a prophet's life, based only on the information we have received in the Noble Qur'an. At the end of each story you will find a list of references to the Qur'an where the story can be found. You might want to look up these references. Extra details and stories, however interesting, have not been added, to be fair to you and to give you as true a picture as possible, based only on the Glorious Qur'an.

The English translations of the Qur'an which have been used in retelling these stories were done by Abdullah Yusuf Ali, Marmaduke Pickthall, Muhammad Asad and Zafar Ishaq Ansari.

The Noble Qur'an, as you know, was revealed to Prophet Muhammad (May the Peace and Blessings of Allah be upon him) and the story of his great life deserves a complete book by itself. Look for his story in Volume Two of *Lives of the Prophets*.

We show respect for Allah by saying *Subhanahu Wa Ta'ala* (How Glorious and Exalted He is!) whenever we say His name. Likewise, we say *Alaihis-Salam* (Peace be upon him) whenever we say the name of any prophet, excepting Prophet Muhammad, Allah's last Messenger, for whom we should say *Sallalla-hu-alaihi-wasallam* (May the Peace and Blessings of Allah be upon him).

Names in these stories

Islamic Names	Judeo/Christian Names
Ben Yamin	Benjamin
Dawood	David
Habil	Abel
Hajar	Hagar
Haroon	Aaron
Hawwa	Eve
Ibraheem	Abraham
Isa	Jesus
Ishaq	Isaac
Ismaeel	Ishmael
Jalut	Saul
Lut	Lot
Maryam	Mary
Musa	Moses
Nuh	Noah
Qabil	Cain
Sulaiman	Solomon
Talut	Goliath
Yahya	John the Baptist
Yaqoob	Jacob
Yunus	Jonah
Yusuf	Joseph
Zulkifl	Ezekial

Key to the Quranic References:
In order to make it easier for the reader to look up the relevant passages in the Qur'an, specific Qur'anic references have been listed at the end of each chapter. The *Surah* number is given first, followed by the numbers of particular *Ayahs* (verses). Thus, in 2:41, '2' refers to the second *Surah* (*Al-Baqrah*), '41' is the particular *Ayah* (verse) which contains the reference.

From Beginning to End

Who made it all?

Heavens above,
Earth below,
Stars in the sky,
The winds that blow,
Mountains and valleys
Where rivers flow,
And the rain that brings life
To the seeds we sow,
Gardens and vineyards
And fields of wheat,
Flowers for beauty
And honey that's sweet,
Grapes, olives, date palms,
The fruits we eat,
Milk for the little ones
And cattle for meat;
All of the creatures
Large and small,
Some creep on the ground
And some stand tall,
Sunrise and set
While songbirds call,
A world of wonders:
Who made it all?

Creation of Heavens and Earth

Where did it all come from? Where did the first animals and birds come from? And the plants? Who made the mountains? The deserts? The oceans? The water to drink? The air to breathe? Everything in the world is organized and interconnected. How did it happen?

When Allah says 'Be', it is. That is how it was in the beginning when everything began from nothing. He made the heavens and the earth, and all that is between them. And that is how it still is as creation keeps growing and changing.

Allah raised the heavens high with sun, moon and stars perfectly organized and perfectly beautiful. Light and energy come from the sun. The moon keeps changing its shape, keeping track of the months and the years. Each star follows its own path across the skies.

On earth, like a veil, the night draws over the day. The night is dark, a time for rest, and then the day comes again when light helps us to see. Day after night, night after day, day and night follow each other as the seasons change.

Allah sends rain to the earth from the sky. It soaks the soil and the water travels through springs in the earth. And then Allah causes all varieties of plants to grow, with many different colours, producing all kinds of food to eat.

There are many kinds of animals, all in pairs, male and female. Some have backbones, others do not. Some are covered with fur, some with scales, some with feathers and others with a shell. Each animal is suited to the place it lives, and animals live everywhere—in the sea, on high mountains, on the grasslands, in the jungle and in the desert. The cattle—the sheep, goats, camels and oxen—are especially helpful for people, giving them milk to drink, meat to eat, wool, hair and leather for clothing, and they carry heavy loads.

Allah gave shape to all things He made, and He made the shapes beautiful.

Power over all things

Allah sees everything that enters earth and comes from the earth, what comes down from heaven and what goes up to heaven. He has complete command over everything. He adds to creqtion as He pleases.

Allah made different beings. He made angels who serve Him in heaven and celebrate the praises of Allah. They are His messengers, with wings—two, three or four pairs of wings. And He made jinns, the invisible spirits, from pure fire that gave no smoke.

Creation of man

Allah said to the angels, 'I am setting on earth a viceroy. He will have power to choose how he will live.' The angels said, 'Will you put someone there who will cause trouble on earth? All the while, we praise You and glorify Your holy name.' He said to them, 'I know what you do not know.' He said, 'When I have made him, in the right shape, and breathed My spirit into him, you shall bow down before him'.

And Allah created the first man. He moulded him into shape from clay. The man was bare and alone. The man's name was Adam. Allah then taught Adam and gave him understanding about many things. Adam learned the names of things, all about their nature and qualities.

Bow down!

Then Allah placed the things before the angels and asked the angels, 'Tell me about these things, and We'll see if you are right.'

The angels said, 'Glory to You. We don't know anything on our own. We only know what You have taught us. In truth it is You who are perfect in knowledge and wisdom.'

Then Allah said to Adam, 'Tell them about these things.'

When Adam had told them, Allah said to the angels, 'Did I not tell you that I know the secrets of heaven and earth, and I know what you show and what you hide?'

Then He said to the angels, 'Bow down to Adam.'

And the angels bowed down to Adam. But Iblees did not. Iblees was one of the jinns, and he refused to be of those who bowed down. He was rebellious and proud and broke the command of Allah.

Allah asked Iblees, 'What stopped you from bowing down to the one whom

I have created with My Hands? Are you proud? Do you think you are high and mighty?'

Iblees said, 'I am better than him. You made me from fire, and him you moulded into shape from mud.'

Allah said, 'Get down from here. It is not for you to be proud here. Get out, for you are a mean creature. The curse shall be on you till the Day of Judgment.'

Satan's plan

The jinn named Iblees had been rejected by Allah. Iblees was very disappointed. His name 'Iblees' means 'someone utterly in despair'. There was another name for Iblees: Shaytan, or Satan. Satan means evil. Iblees was so helpless that all he could do was be rebellious. He knew that with his many hidden powers as a jinn, he could do terrible things in secret.

So Iblees said, 'Oh my God. Give me some time, till the day the dead are raised up.'

Allah said, 'Yes, you have that time, till that day comes.'

Iblees said, 'Because You have thrown me out, I will lie in wait for people on Your straight Way. Then I will attack them from all sides, from front of them, behind them, from the right and from the left. I will make what is wrong seem right to them, and I will put them all in the wrong. I will take some of Your servants and they will follow me, as if they were marked off to be for myself. I will lead them in the wrong way and I will make them want to have things that are really worth nothing. I will make them become slaves to superstitions. I will order them to do things to harm and disturb the pure, beautiful nature You have created.'

Allah said, 'Go your way. But be warned. You will all land in hell. Lead away whoever you can with your secret voice. Attack them with your powers. Share riches and children with them. And make your promises to them.'

Satan said to Allah, ' And You will find that most of them will not be thankful to You for Your Mercies.'

Allah said, 'Get out from here. You shall have no power over my servants, except those who put themselves in the wrong and follow you. If any of them follow you, I will fill hell with all of them. There are seven gates, and a special group will go in through each gate.'

And so this is how Iblees began with a lie. He stepped lower and lower. He showed what he was: he was proud, jealous, disobediant, dishonest and he thought only about himself.

Life in Jannah

Allah then turned to Adam and created a partner for him. This was his wife, Hawwa. Allah created both the man and the woman in the best of forms.

And Allah said, 'Oh Adam! You and your mate shall live in Jannah, this wonderful garden, and enjoy its good things as you wish. Eat of the bountiful things here, wherever and whenever you wish. There is enough in Jannah to meet your needs, so you will not go hungry, nor go naked, nor suffer from thirst, nor from the sun's heat.'

'But one thing: Do not approach this tree, or you will run into harm and do wrong. Oh Adam! Be careful. Iblees is an enemy to you and your mate. So be warned. Do not let him get you both out of Jannah, so that you become unhappy.'

Adam and his wife lived in purity, beauty and goodness. They had a very good life in Jannah.

Temptations

Satan began to whisper suggestions to Adam and his wife. He said, 'Oh Adam! Shall I lead you to the Tree of Eternity and to a kingdom that never decays?' He brought into their minds all kinds of ideas that had been hidden before. Satan swore to them both that he was their sincere advisor.

Adam and his wife were tempted.

Satan said, 'Your God did forbid you to eat from this tree only to prevent you from becoming angels, or from living forever.'

He finally persuaded them to disobey Allah's command. They ate of the tree that Allah had forbidden them.

When they tasted fruit from the tree, they knew immediately that what they had done was wrong. They wanted to hide in Jannah and began to use leaves to cover themselves.

And Allah called to them, 'Did I not forbid you that tree? And did I not tell you that Satan was your enemy?'

They cried, 'Our God! We have done something terribly wrong.'

Now they knew about evil. They were guilty and they were ashamed. They continued crying to Allah, 'If you do not forgive us and do not give us Your Mercy, we shall certainly be lost!'

Go down!

Allah commanded, 'Go down. You will from now on be enemies to each other. The earth will be your place to live for a while. That is where you must make your living and that is where shall die. But You shall, eventually be, taken out from there.'

Then Allah turned towards Adam, for Allah is full of forgiveness and most merciful, and gave Adam words of inspiration and spiritual knowledge. And Allah said, 'Go down from here, and when a message comes to you from Me, follow My guidance. Whoever follows My message will not lose his way. Followers should not be afraid, and should not worry.'

And then Allah told them about the life after death. 'Those who believe in Me and do what is right will live in Jannah forever. Those who turn away from my message and do not accept the signs that I send them will end up in the fires of hell forever. Those who go to Jannah will be in wonderful gardens with streams of clear flowing water. There they will never get tired. And they will never, ever, be asked to leave.'

Life on earth

So Adam and Hawwa had to leave their wonderful life in Jannah and went down to live on earth. What could they eat? How could they keep warm? Where could

they find safe places to sleep? They had to work hard to live, day after day. Every day they became very tired because of all their work. It wasn't easy to live on earth.

Adam and his wife had two sons. The eldest was named Qabil and the youngest, Habil. This was the first family on earth, and Adam taught them about Allah.

Qabil and Habil wanted to present a sacrifice to Allah. When they had made their sacrifice, Allah accepted the sacrifice of the younger brother, but not of Qabil. Qabil was jealous of Habil. Qabil was so jealous and hated his younger brother so much that he said to him, 'Be sure that I will kill you.'

Habil then said to his elder brother, 'Allah surely accepts the sacrifice of people who do what is right. If you raise your hand to kill me, it is not my right to do the same to you. I fear Allah, who takes care of the worlds. Remember what happens to those who do wrong.'

Qabil was filled with anger. He was so angry that he murdered his brother. And by murdering him, he became one of the lost ones.

Then Allah sent a raven to Qabil with a message. The raven scratched on the ground, as if to show him something. Qabil felt very bad. He felt that he needed to hide what he had done. 'Woe is me!' he said. 'I wasn't even able to be like this raven, who shows me what to do!'

Then Qabil became sorry for what he had done. He had killed a person—his brother—his good brother. And then the raven had to show him that he had not even buried the body.

Satan had taken Qabil to be his follower, and Qabil had been misled from the right way.

Because of what happened between these two brothers, Allah made it clear that if anyone killed another person it would be as if he had killed all people. And if anyone saved a life, it would be as if he had saved the lives of all people.

Messages from Allah

Many, many years passed and the earth became filled with people.

As He had promised, Allah sent messages to guide people on earth, to show them the right way. Allah told His messengers, 'Warn man, that there is no God but I.' The angel Jibrael was one of the most honourable of messengers, with high rank before the Lord of the Throne. Mikael was another. So Jibrael and Mikael and other angels carried the messages to earth. With Allah's will they brought them to people's hearts, along with the spirit of faith and truth.

Allah said that angels are sent down to help the people believe. For those who believe and live in the right way, angels come down from time to time to strengthen their hearts and tell them not to be afraid. 'We are your protectors in this life and the hereafter.' The angels also pray for forgiveness for the wrong things that are done on earth.

Certain good people, at different times in history, were chosen to receive a special message from Allah, and they were to warn others and teach them more about Allah. These men were called prophets.

Prophet Nuh told his people to change their bad ways and remember Allah. The people didn't want to listen to him and said he was crazy. But Prophet Nuh warned them that they would have a terrible end if they did not stop the evil things they were doing. He also warned them to believe in Allah, who had all power on earth. Only a few people believed the message. Allah then sent a terrible flood which destroyed all the non-believers. The great flood washed away everything on earth that was bad. The few people who had listened to Prophet Nuh were saved.

Prophet Ibraheem was called by Allah to leave the faith of his fathers and settle in a new land, along with his nephew, Lut. Many temptations came to Ibraheem, but his faith in Allah was strong and he stayed on the right path. Prophet Ibraheem had sons named Ismaeel and Ishaq. Ishaq had a son named Yaqoob, who had a son named Yusuf. All these men who came after Prophet Ibraheem were prophets too. Allah filled their hearts with wisdom, gave them power and made them leaders among their people.

Prophet Musa, after several generations, became the leader of the Children of Israel, the name for the descendents of Prophet Yaqoob. Allah gave Prophet Musa a book of His Law called the Torah to guide the Children of Israel and keep them on the right path.

In later times, Allah sent Prophet Isa to the Children of Israel. The book of guidance which Prophet Isa received from Allah was called the Bible.

Prophet Muhammad (May the Peace and Blessings of Allah be upon him) was a descendent of Ismaeel, son of Ibraheem. The angel Jibraeel brought the Qur'an to Prophet Muhammad (May the Peace and Blessings of Allah be upon him). This was the greatest message of all, and Prophet Muhammad, (May the Peace and Blessings of Allah be upon him), was the last and the greatest prophet of all.

There were many other prophets that brought Allah's message to different people in different times. Some people would listen to the message the prophets brought and they would believe, change their ways and follow on the right path.

There was once a group of jinns quietly listening to the Qur'an. 'Listen in silence!' they said. When the reading was finished, they returned to their people, and said to them, 'We have heard a wonderful Book. It guides to the Truth and to the straight path. Some foolish ones among us used to tell lies against Allah. But no man or spirit should say anything untrue against Allah. Can't they see that Allah, who created the heavens and the earth, has power over all things?'

But many people did not listen to the messages from Allah. They lived badly, doing wrong things and not remembering Allah who had made them. They made fun of the prophets who came to warn them, mocking them and their words. And Satan, the leader of the evil jinns, misled many people to the wrong path.

The Day of Judgement

Allah had told Adam that he and his people would live on earth for some time and die there, and at an appointed time, those who believed and did what is right would be admitted to the gardens of Jannah to live there forever.

When that appointed time will be is hidden from people, but a day will come when all people will be raised from the dead and judged for what they have done in their lives on earth. Because Allah knows everything, all deeds and thoughts will be recalled clearly. Everything that they have done in their lives has been written down.

It will not be a happy day for people on the wrong path. When they see their Book of Deeds, they will say, 'Woe to us! What a book this is! It leaves out nothing, great or small. Everything that we have done is here.' And when they see the angels, they will say, 'Oh! I wish I had taken a straight path with the prophet. I should have never taken Satan for a friend. He led me astray from the message of Allah after it had come to me!'

On that day, Allah will ask the angels, 'Did these men worship you?'

The angels will say, 'No, they worshipped the jinns, and most of them believed in them.'

Satan, the leader of the evil jinns, will say to people, 'It was Allah who gave you a promise of truth. I too promised, but I didn't keep my promise to you. I had no power to do anything but call to you. But you listened to me. Then do not blame me but blame yourselves. I cannot listen to your cries and you cannot listen to my cries.'

And a man will say, 'Oh my God! Why have you raised me up blind? I could see before.'

Then Allah will tell him, 'This is how you were, when the signs of my message came to you. You turned away from them. On this day you will be treated in the same way.'

People themselves will see whether they are on the right path or the wrong path. Allah will send them to the right, to the Gardens of Jannah, or to the left to the fires of hell.

Forever and ever

Jannah is the eternal home for those who have believed in Allah and have stayed on the right path. It is the most beautiful garden, full of wonderful things, where everyone will be near to Allah.

Rivers flow beneath the Garden, and it is filled with every kind of fruit. Everyone will have everything that they need. They will never get tired. Allah has said that lofty mansions, one above another, have been built. Believers will be joined with their families and their friends, with those who followed the right path in faith. And they will never be asked to leave. Everyone will live in purity and beauty and peace forever and ever.

This story is found in the Noble Qur'an in many different Surahs:

2:30-9,53,97-8,117; 3:15,198; 4:117-20; 5:30-5; 6:94-100,130-1,141-4; 7:11-31,54,200; 8:29; 10:4-6; 14:22;
15:7-11,17,26-44,85; 16:2,3; 17:61-5; 18:48-50; 20:115-26; 21:16-7; 23:12-4,18-22; 24:21; 25:21-5;
26:98,193; 27:64; 29:19-20; 32:4; 34:41; 35:1,6,27; 36:60,82; 38:71-85; 39:5,6,19-20; 40:57,60-8;
41:30-1; 42:5; 44:46-55; 45:22; 46:3,29-32; 51:56; 52:7-10,17-25; 53:21; 55:14-5; 57:4-6;
70:4; 72:1-15; 74:1-5; 79:24-33; 81:19; 82:10-2; 95:3.

Prophet Nuh

(Peace be Upon Him)

and the Flood

A world of non-believers

Many, many years ago, there was a time when most people did not worship Allah. They did not believe that Allah had made the world and everything in it. They worshipped things like the sun, the moon, the stars or animals like the cow, the lion, the snake or the eagle. They were superstitious. They did not think that Allah knew everything that they did. They did not think that it was wrong to do bad things.

During that time, Allah chose a good man named Nuh to tell the people to change their ways. Nuh went to his own people to warn them. He said to them, 'You should be good. You should worship Allah. I am afraid that Allah will punish you for all the bad things that you do.'

The leaders of the people who did not believe in Allah said, 'Nuh is a man just like us. He doesn't really know anything. If Allah wanted to send messengers He could have sent down angels. We've never heard of such a thing in the past.'

And some of the people said, 'He's only a crazy fellow. Wait and have some patience with him for a time.'

'Oh my people! I'm not crazy. Can't you see that this message is a warning from Allah? I want to help you, but I can't make you believe,' Nuh replied.

The people told each other, 'Don't turn away from your gods. Keep worshipping your idols.' They had many idols. One was Wadd. Another was Suwa. And then there were Yaguth, Ya'uq and Nasr. Many of the people were misled by others, to the wrong path of life.

A faithful messenger

Nuh spoke to the people in groups and he spoke to people when they were alone. He said to them, 'Ask Allah to forgive you.' But they did not listen to Nuh. They listened to their own leaders or to people who were rich. And things got worse.

'What's wrong with you?' Nuh asked them, 'Why don't you look to Allah for kindness, when you see everything that He has made around you? And He has made everything in different stages. Don't you see that Allah has made the seven heavens, one on top of the other? And made the moon a light in their midst and made the sun like a wonderful lamp? Allah brought you from the earth, growing in stages, and in the end He will return you to the earth, and then raise you up again when He calls. And see how He has spread the earth like a carpet for you, so that you can easily move around everywhere you want to go.'

The people tried to find reasons for not listening to Nuh's message. The leaders of the people said, 'Why should we listen to you, when we see that it is only the lowly people that follow you? They follow you because they don't know any better.'

Nuh told them, 'I will not send away any people who believe. Who would help them if I sent them away? And how do I know what they do? I tell you - I don't have the treasures of Allah. I do not know any secrets, and I am not from another world. And as for all these people whom you don't like who follow me, Allah knows what they do. Who knows? - Allah might give them everything that is good. I cannot say bad things about them. Allah knows best what's inside them.'

The people don't listen

The people said, 'Oh Nuh, you have argued with us, and you've made this go on for a long time. You said we would be punished if we didn't change our ways. Now what can you do? Or do we have to call you a liar?'

Nuh told them, 'I am sent only to warn everyone, that you should be good and worship Allah. Allah will bring disaster on you if He wills, and then you won't be able to do anything about it. And then, even if I'd want to help you, I couldn't.'

They said, 'If you don't stop this Nuh, you will be stoned to death!' And the people made plots against Nuh.

Nuh said to them, 'If you have a plan against me, tell us all, so no one will be in the dark. Then tell me what you want to do with me.'

Then Nuh prayed to Allah, 'Oh my God! I can't win! I have called to my people night and day! What I say just makes them go further away. And every time I have told them that You might forgive them, they have only put their fingers in their ears and surrounded themselves more tightly with whatever it is that they're doing. They've become stubborn and are lost in their pride. And now they have a tremendous plot against me. My people have really rejected me. I have called them to You openly and secretly, and they continually refuse to listen. I invited them toYou at night and during the day, but the people rejected my invitation. Judge between me and them, and save me and the believers who are with me.'

Building the ark

Nuh was then given a message from Allah: 'No more of your people will believe. So don't worry about the others who don't listen. But go now and build an ark with my instructions and help. There will be a flood, and when that happens you will go on board with pairs of every kind of animal. Take your family with you, except for those who do not believe. And don't ask me any more about the people who are in a bad way, because they will be washed away in the flood. When you have all gone into the ark, say 'Praise be to Allah, who has saved us from the people who do what is wrong.'

Nuh immediately started to build the ark. It was made of broad planks of wood and made watertight with palm fibre.

Every time the leaders of his people passed him working on the boat, they made fun of him.

Nuh said to them, 'If you make fun of us now, later on we'll have our turn. We will look down on you in the same way. You'll soon know who will have the punishment that will last forever.'

Nuh kept building. Finally the ark was finished.

The flood

Then there was a command from Allah. It started to rain.
It rained and it rained, and it kept on raining.

Nuh said, '*Bismillah.* Go in the ark, whether or not it's moving.'

So Nuh's family, other believers and all different kinds of creatures went into the ark. Then water started gushing out from springs in the earth. The water from the sky above and the water from the earth below met, and it was a huge flood. The ark floated on waves that were as high as hills.

Nuh's son

Nuh called out to his son, who had not come along with the rest, 'Oh my son, come on board with us and don't be with the non-believers.'

The son answered his father, 'I will go up on some mountain. It will save me from the water.'

Nuh said: 'On this day, nothing can save anyone from the command of Allah except those for whom Allah has mercy.'

The waves came between them. Nuh called to Allah and said, 'Oh my God! My son is of my family! What has happened to him?'

Allah said,'Oh Nuh! He is not of your family, because he does things that are not good. So don't ask me about him.'

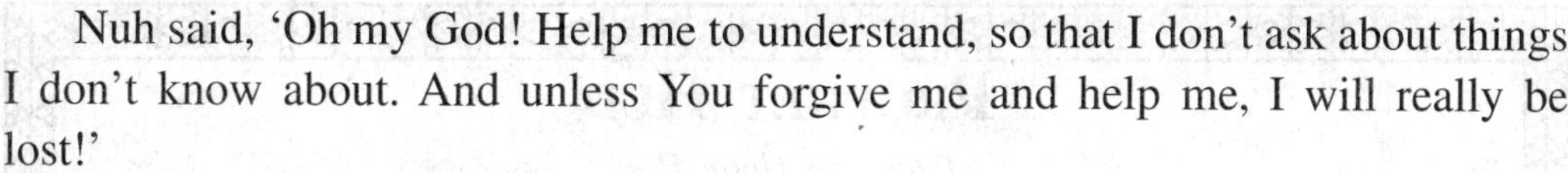

Nuh said, 'Oh my God! Help me to understand, so that I don't ask about things I don't know about. And unless You forgive me and help me, I will really be lost!'

Nuh's son was among those people who drowned in the water of the flood.

The end of the flood

Allah watched and the ark floated under His care.

Then finally the word went out:

'Oh earth! Swallow up the water!

Oh sky! Hold back your rain!'

And the rain stopped and the water went down, and the flood was over.

The ark stopped on Mount Judi and the word went out:

'Away with those who do wrong!'

A clean world

The word came: 'Oh Nuh! Come out of the ark, and live in peace.'

So Nuh and the believers and all the animals came out of the ark.

Peace be upon Nuh among all beings. Peace be upon Nuh among all the worlds. Everything in the world had been washed clean. The great flood had washed away everything that was bad.

This story about Prophet Nuh, who lived among his people for 950 years, is found in the Noble Qur'an in many different Surahs:

7:59-64; 11:25-49; 23:23-30; 26:105-22; 37:75-82; 54:9-15;
10:71-3; 21:76-7; 25:37; 29:14-5; 51:46; 69:11-2;
71:1-28.

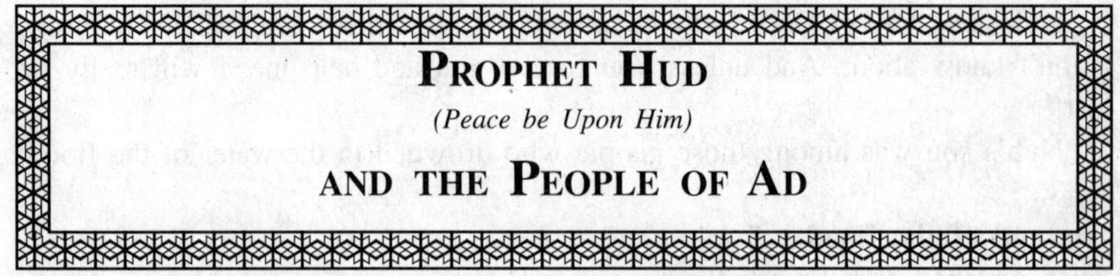

PROPHET HUD
(Peace be Upon Him)
AND THE PEOPLE OF AD

The people of Ad

Many, many years after the great flood had washed the world clean, the people of Ad lived in the vast lands of southern Arabia. They were named after a man whose name was Ad. Ad could trace his family all the way back to the Prophet Nuh. Ad's father was Aus, who was the son of Aram, who was the son of Sam, who was the son of Nuh.

The Ad were intelligent people. Allah had given them special abilities to use their ears, eyes, hearts and minds. Not only could they see and hear very well, which helped them to live in the desert lands, they had many ideas about how to build their towns, grow crops, raise animals and live comfortably in the desert. So the Ad became strong and wealthy people.

The Ad lived in the long and winding tracts of land in the sandhills called *ahqaf*. There were many springs of water in the *ahqaf*, and so they could irrigate this land. They had many large gardens. The crops were good. They had large flocks of animals. They built beautiful houses and other fine buildings. Their city, Iram, was known as the place of many pillars. On every high place in their country they built a landmark.

A message of warning from Hud

The Ad were rich people. They were strong and powerful in the land. But the Ad did not thank Allah for all good things He had given them. They forgot the story of Prophet Nuh and the flood. Many of the people even forgot all about Allah. They worshipped idols and many other things in their prosperous lives. They built houses as if they were going to live forever and would never die.

Then Allah chose Hud from among the Ad to warn his own people.

Hud said, 'Oh my people! Worship Allah! You have no other God but Him! You're just inventing your other gods.'

The leaders of the people who did not believe in Allah said, 'Ah! We see that you are foolish!'

Hud said to them, 'Oh my people! I am no fool! Ask your God to forgive you. Change your ways and turn to Him.'

They said, 'Oh Hud! You have not brought us a clear sign and we are not the ones to leave our gods just at your word. And we shall not believe in you.'

Hud told them, 'Allah will send rain pouring down from the skies to you. He has freely given you everything that you have. He has given you cattle and sons and gardens and springs of water. You are strong and He will make you stronger. Really, if you don't change, I am afraid for all of you. There will be punishment for you one day. So don't go back to your bad ways of life.'

The leaders of the non-believers said to Hud, 'We think you are a liar!'

Hud said, 'I am a messenger from the God of the Worlds. I am not asking you for anything. I have only come to warn you because my God has sent me. I am telling you the truth. You can trust me.' The people said, 'Well, we won't exactly call you a liar. Maybe some of our gods have taken you and made you into a fool!'

Hud said, 'Allah is my witness. And you are also witnesses—you can see that I worship no other gods beside Allah. I put my trust in Allah, my God and your God. There is not a moving creature that He doesn't control. His complete Power over everything is just like when you hold the forelock of a horse's mane and you have complete control over the horse.'

Non-believers

The people asked, 'Do you come to tell us that we should worship just Allah, and give up what our fathers taught us?'

Hud replied, 'Yes! Do you wonder that a message of warning from your God comes to you through me, a man of your own people? Just remember—you follow after the people of Nuh, and you are very important among the nations. Remember the help you have received from Allah, so that you have become rich and powerful.'

They asked again, 'You have come to turn us away from our gods?'

Hud said, 'Are you arguing with me over things which you have made up, you and your fathers, without permission and authority from Allah? Will you not fear Allah?'

They said, 'It is the same to us whether you preach to us or not. You're telling us just the same old things and we are not the ones who will receive pains and punishments.' So they turned away from him.

Hud spoke to his people again, 'I see that you are a people in ignorance! If you turn away, at least I have given you the message with which I was sent to you. After you, other people will follow.'

The end of the Ad

The people taunted Hud, 'You threatened us with disaster. Bring it to us then, if you tell the truth!'

He said, 'Your God is already angry with you. Only Allah knows when the disaster will come. So just wait. I am with you, also waiting.'

One day they saw their punishment coming towards them in the shape of a cloud crossing the sky. When they saw the cloud coming toward their valleys, they said, 'This cloud will give us rain.'

Hud said, 'No, it is the disaster for which you were asking! The cloud comes with a terrible wind that brings your punishment. It will destroy everything by the command of its God!'

Then the disaster struck the Ad. A terrible wind blew for a whole week. By the eighth morning there was nothing to be seen but the ruins of their fine houses. Their houses looked as if they were uprooted hollow palm trees.

This was the punishment for people whom Allah had given riches and power. He had given them many great gifts, especially the abilities to use their senses. But all of this was of no use to them—how well they could hear with their ears, see with their eyes, understand with their hearts and think with their minds, when they kept on turning away from the signs of Allah. They were on the wrong path, worshipping the wrong things, doing bad things and what they believed wasn't true.

So when Allah sent the disaster to the Ad to destroy them, only Hud and those who believed his message were saved. Those who did not believe and turned away from the signs of Allah were not saved.

This story of the Prophet Hud is found in the Noble Qur'an in the following Surahs:

7:65-72;	23:31-43;	27:45-53;	69:4-8,
11:50-60;	26:123-40;	46:21-6;	89:7.

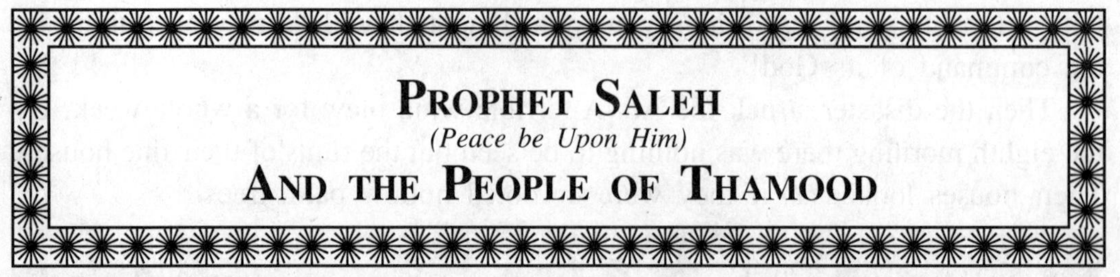

Prophet Saleh
(Peace be Upon Him)
And the People of Thamood

The people of Thamood

Many, many years after the great flood had washed the world clean, the Thamood lived in the northwestern lands of Arabia. They were named after a man whose name was Thamood, who could trace his family back to Prophet Nuh. Thamood's father was 'Abir, who was the son of Sam, who was the son of Nuh.

The people of Thamood were the cousins of the people of Ad. The Ad lived in the desert lands of southern Arabia, where they had irrigated their lands and grown food crops. They had raised huge flocks of animals and built beautiful cities. The Thamood knew that the Ad had been rich people and that they had not worshipped Allah. They knew that the Ad had been destroyed because they had not believed in Allah.

The land of the Thamood was made of sand dunes, vast rocky hills and wide valleys where good gardens and crops would grow. They followed the Ad in building up big and beautiful towns. They were masters of stone and hollowed out rocks in the valley to make buildings that grew right out of the mountains. They made wonderful carvings on their buildings and in their streets.

Some of the Thamood believed in Allah. But many people, especially those who were wealthy and powerful, were proud and they did not worship Allah.

Change your ways!

There was a good man among the Thamood whose name was Saleh. Many people thought that he would become their leader. Allah chose Saleh to be a messenger to his own people.

Saleh said, 'Oh my people! Worship Allah. You have no other God but Him. Allah made you from the earth and settled you on the earth. Remember how Allah made you follow the people of Ad, and gave you places to live in the land. You built for yourselves palaces and castles on the open plains and carved homes for yourselves in the mountains. Are you safe enjoying everything you have here? You have gardens and springs of water and fields of corn. You can grow date palms with fruit so heavy that the tree nearly breaks. And you can certainly carve beautiful houses out of the sides of the rocky mountains with great skill. But you must fear Allah. Obey my message and don't be like those who spend too much and are wasteful. Don't be like those who do bad things in the land and don't change their ways.'

Some of the people listened to Saleh and believed his message. Others did not.

The people disagree

The people of Thamood became divided into two groups, quarrelling with each other.

The leaders of the people who did not believe in Saleh's message claimed they would not be judged in life after they died. They told the people, 'Saleh is just a man like everyone else, he eats what you eat and drinks what you drink. If you obey a man like yourselves, you will surely be lost. Does he promise you that after you die and have become dust and bones, you will be brought up again? What a promise! There is nothing but our life in this world. We live and we shall die. But we shall never be raised up again. He is telling lies.'

Saleh said to the people, 'Oh my people! Why do some of you choose the bad over the good? Why are you so quickly becoming worse and worse?'

The people said to Saleh, 'You are speaking like a mad man.'

Saleh told them, 'If only you ask forgiveness from Allah, and turn to Him to live good lives, you have some hope, for my God is always near, ready to answer.'

The people said, 'Oh Saleh! You were one of us! We hoped until now that you would become our leader. Are you now forbidding us to worship what our fathers worshipped? We really don't like what you're asking us to do. We think this is a bad sign for you and those who are with you.'

Saleh said, 'Your bad sign is with Allah. Yes, you are a people under trial.'

The proud people did not want to listen to Saleh's message.

Saleh said, 'Oh my people! Can't you see? I myself have a clear sign from my God and He helps me. If I then disobey Him, who can help me against Allah? All you are trying to do is get me in deep trouble.'

The leaders of the people who were proud said to those who were lowly, 'Do you know that Saleh really is a messenger from his God?'

They said, 'We really believe in the message which has been sent through him.'

The proud ones said, 'We don't believe it.'

The sign of a camel

The people continued to argue with Saleh. They said to him, 'You are a man just like us. Then bring us a sign if you are telling the truth.' And they asked for a camel to be born out of the rock.

Saleh knew that Allah had the power to do anything. He called on Allah and the camel appeared.

Saleh then showed them the camel and said to the astonished people, 'Oh my people! Now a clear sign has come to you from your God. This female camel from Allah is a sign for you. He created her for you by His Power. So you must

respect this camel. Let her graze freely in the land. Let her go wherever she wants. Let her drink water, just as you can drink water. Let no harm come to her. If something happens to her you will receive a quick and terrible punishment.'

But the people didn't care. They became annoyed with the camel. In defiance, they decided that they would get rid of this camel and went against the order from Allah. Spitefully people said, 'Oh Saleh, if you are the messenger of Allah, bring about your threats.' With that the people tied the legs of the camel so that she could not move around.

When Saleh heard what had happened, he was very disappointed. And then Saleh said to them, 'Enjoy yourselves in your homes for three days. Then will come your ruin. You will see that this is a promise that will certainly come true.'

After that some of the people became sorry for what they had done.

Plots against Saleh

In the city there were nine men of a family who did terrible things in the land. They would not change their ways. They did not want to hear Saleh's message and made plots against him.

They made a plan to kill him. In their meeting they said, 'We all swear an oath that we shall make a secret attack on Saleh and his people. It will be at night.

Later when his family is looking for the murderers and asks questions, we will all say "We were not there when they were killed, and we are telling the truth".' All of them promised each other they would tell the lie. This is how they plotted and planned.

But Allah also had a plan, and the nine men did not know it.

The end of the Thamood

In three days their punishment took them by surprise. There was a terrible blast. And then there was an earthquake. Before the morning, they were lying dead in the ruins of their homes.

Saleh left them and said, 'O' my people! I did bring you the message from Allah. I gave you good advice, but you don't listen to good advice.'

It was as if the people of Thamood had never lived and prospered there. Saleh was saved from the terror of that day, as well as those who believed him.

This story of the Prophet Saleh is found in the Noble Qur'an in the following Surahs:

7:73-9;	23:31-43;	69:4-7;
11:61-8;	26:141-59;	89:9.

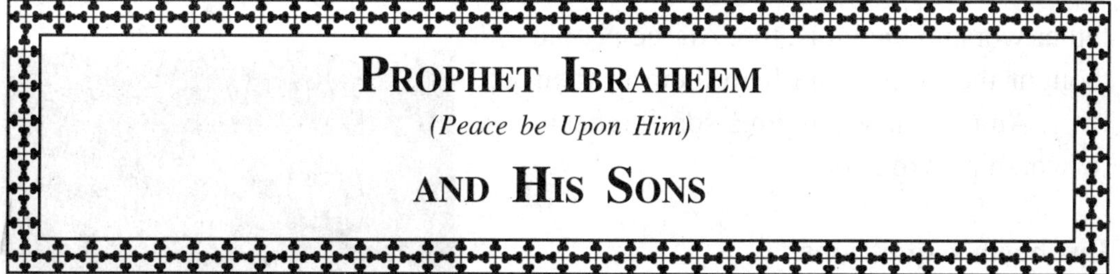

PROPHET IBRAHEEM
(Peace be Upon Him)
AND HIS SONS

Growing up in Ur

Ur of the Chaldees was on the Euphrates River. It was busy with many people coming and going. There were big bazaars where people were selling and buying.

There were schools for children. There were places where people studied about many things in the world. Some people studied the sky at night and knew all about the moon and the stars. Some of them worshipped the heavenly bodies.

There was a noble man in Ur whose name was Aazar, who had a son named Ibraheem. Ibraheem grew up learning many things from his father and his teachers. He was especially interested in learning about the stars and how they moved across the sky at night.

Most of the people of Ur worshipped idols. Ibraheem would see the people bowing down before the idols and knew those statues of stone couldn't hear or

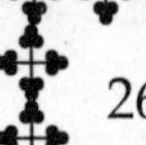

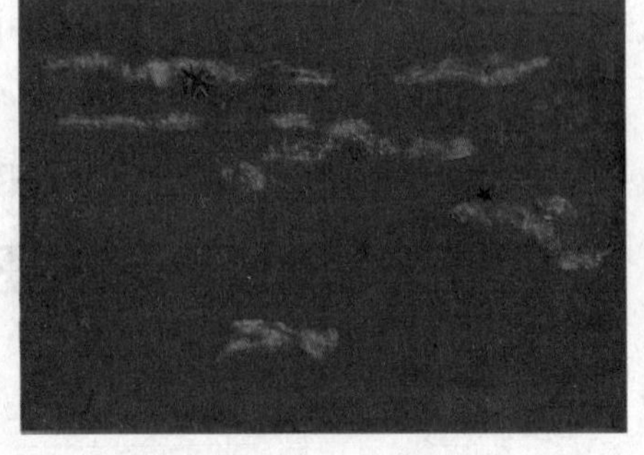

speak or do anything. Ibraheem watched his father worship the idols, too. All the people thought the idols could help them in their lives. And Aazar wanted his son Ibraheem to worship them, too.

Ibraheem's questions

Ibraheem asked many questions. He kept wondering: Who made the sky and the earth? Who arranges all the stars in the sky? Who brings out the day and who brings the night? Who controls everything? Ibraheem learned as much as he could about the world. He kept watching and studying the power and laws of the sky and the earth. And he asked himself, 'Why do people worship idols? Why do they ask those stone carvings to help them?'

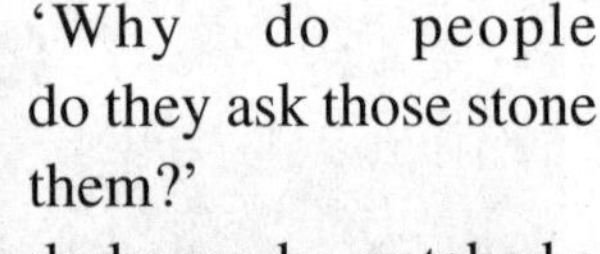

At night, in the darkness, he watched a very bright shining star and said, 'So this is what I can believe in!' But it moved across the sky and set, and then he said, 'I do not love things that set and disappear.'

When he saw the beautiful moon rise in the evenings and watched how its shape kept changing, he said, 'So this is what I can believe in!' But when it set he said, 'Unless my God guides me, I will not understand what is true and I will be lost.'

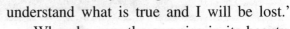

When he saw the sun rise in its beauty, he said, 'So this is what I can believe in! This is the biggest of all.' But the sun set. Ibraheem could not worship something that kept appearing and disappearing.

Ibraheem tried to be honest in everything he did and said and thought. He asked himself, 'What do I really believe? Who is my God?'

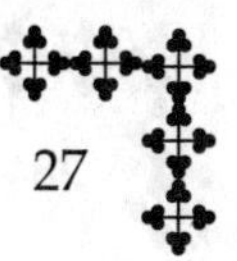

There is one God

Then God guided Ibraheem and taught him the truth. The truth was this: The name of God is Allah, the one God. He is always living and does not die.

The light of Allah is always shining and never dims and never sets. The light of the stars is weak, and morning overcomes it. The light of the moon is weak, and the sun overcomes it. The light of the sun is also weak, clouds can cover it and night overcomes it. Allah has made the sun, the moon, the stars, the earth and all living things. And Allah has made them with a purpose. Allah alone can help.

Allah told Ibraheem to tell other people to worship the one and only God.

Questions for his family

One day Ibraheem said to his father and others in his family, 'What do you worship?'

They said, 'We worship idols. And we take good care of them.'

Ibraheem asked, 'Do they listen to you when you call on them? Do they do you any good?'

They answered, 'No. But our fathers worshipped them. So that is what we do.'

Then Ibraheem asked, 'So do you see what you and your fathers have been worshipping? Why do you ask these stone idols for things when they can't hear or speak? You set offerings of food and drink in front of them! They can't eat or drink! Why do you do this?'

Ibraheem then told them what he believed. 'Your idols are enemies to me. I worship one God. I have set my face towards Allah who made the heavens and the earth. Allah created me and He guides me. He gives me food and drink and when I am sick, He makes me well. He will cause me to die and then to live again. And I pray that He will forgive whatever I have done wrong. I shall never worship anyone except Allah.'

Questions for others

Ibraheem asked some other people a question. 'Do you worship gods that are not real? I see that you have made a big mistake.'

They said, 'Are you joking?'

'Certainly I tell you the truth,' he said. 'Your God is the God of the heavens and the earth, the One who made everything from nothing.'

The people argued with Ibraheem, but he said, ‘Do you come to argue with me about God, when it is God Himself who helped me understand and guided me? I am not afraid of the idols that you worship. Unless my God will make something happen, nothing can happen. My God knows everything. Won’t you understand this? Why should I be afraid of your idols? You worship them without any reason. Which of us, you or I, should be more afraid? Tell me, if you know. It is the people who mix up their beliefs with wrong things, like believing in idols, that should be afraid. People who believe in Allah do not need to be afraid, because they have the right guidance.’

Ibraheem looked at the stars in the night sky and said, ‘In my heart, I am really sick of all this.’

Who makes the sun rise?

The kings who ruled during that time were called Nimrud, and the Nimrud who ruled the city believed he was very powerful. All the people had to bow down before him. When the Nimrud heard that Ibraheem bowed down only before Allah, and no one else, he became angry and sent for Ibraheem.

Nimrud asked Ibraheem, ‘Who is your Lord, Ibraheem?’

Ibraheem answered, ‘Allah is my Lord.’

Then Nimrud asked, ‘Who is Allah, Ibraheem?’

Ibraheem said to him, ‘Allah is the One who gives life and death.’

Nimrud was proud and said, ‘I give life and death.’

To show Ibraheem what he meant, Nimrud had a man brought before him and had him killed. Then he had another man brought before him who had been sentenced to death and let him live. And then Nimrud said, ‘You see, Ibraheem—I give life and I give death. I killed one man, and I gave the other man his life.’

Ibraheem then spoke to Nimrud, ‘But it is Allah who makes the sun rise from the east. Now you make the sun rise from the west.’

Nimrud was confused. What could he say to that?

Smashing the idols

To the people who argued with him, Ibraheem said, ‘I have a plan for your idols. I’ll wait till after you go away and turn your backs on them. Then you will understand me.’

When all the people left to go to a festival, Ibraheem went to the place in the city where the idols were kept. He looked at the rows of idols and said, 'Why don't you eat these offerings of food and drink set in front of you? Can't you hear? What is the matter with you that you don't speak?'

The stone carvings didn't answer.

Then Ibraheem smashed the idols to pieces. He only left one unbroken—the biggest one. It looked as if there had been a fight among the idols and the biggest one had smashed all the rest.

When the people returned and saw what had happened, they said, 'Who has done this to our gods? He must be someone who doesn't believe.'

Those who had heard Ibraheem before said, 'We heard a young man talking about the idols. His name is Ibraheem.'

Then the people had a meeting. They decided that they would continue to believe in their idols and that they must punish Ibraheem.

They found Ibraheem and brought him before the crowd of angry people. They asked Ibraheem, 'Are you the one who did this to our gods, Ibraheem?'

Ibraheem answered, 'This was done by—,' and pointing to the one idol that was still standing, he said, 'This is their biggest one. Ask it, if it can answer you.' The people were confused, and said to Ibraheem, 'You know that these idols do not speak.'

When they said this, Ibraheem asked them another question: 'So then why do you worship such useless things? They're no good for you. You are worshipping things that you yourselves have carved! And it is Allah who has made you. Don't you have any sense?'

Many people were very angry with Ibraheem. They said, 'Burn him. Throw him in a fire.'

The cool fire

The people built a huge fire. When it was blazing hot, they threw Ibraheem in the fire to burn him.

But Allah was taking care of Ibraheem. Allah said to the fire, 'Be cool and comfortable for Ibraheem' and the fire obeyed. It did not harm Ibraheem. Again, the people were confused.

The people were still angry with Ibraheem. Even though they had seen how Allah protected him from the fire, they did not listen to Ibraheem. They plotted and made secret plans against him. But Allah took care of Ibraheem and the people failed in their plans.

Time to move

Ibraheem said to his father, 'Oh my father! Why do you worship things which can't hear, can't see, and are of no good for you? I know things that you don't understand. So follow me. I will guide you to a way that is straight and perfect. Oh my father, do not worship Satan, because Satan is a rebel against Allah. I am afraid that Allah will punish you.'

His father said to him, 'Do you hate my gods, Ibraheem? If you keep on like this, I will beat you. Just leave me alone.'

Ibraheem then said to his father: 'I wish you peace. I will turn away from all of you and your idols. I will call on my God. Perhaps with my prayer to my God I will be blessed.'

After that Allah gave Ibraheem a message to leave his people. He should move to another land with his nephew Lut.

So Ibraheem and Lut took their families and moved away. Ibraheem left his father, his home and all the people he knew. He left the land where he had grown up, and he trusted Allah to be his guide.

Ibraheem and Lut moved to another land far away. This new place was where Allah wanted them to live. Here they could tell other people about Allah.

The four birds

All his life, Ibraheem had been asking questions and learning as much as he

could. As he grew older, he tried to understand more about life and death and the life after death. Allah was teaching him and filled his heart with wisdom and love.

One day, Ibraheem prayed to Allah, 'My God! Show me how you give life to the dead.'

Allah asked him, 'Don't you believe in life after death?'

Ibraheem said, 'Yes, I do. But show me, just to satisfy my heart and mind.'

Allah then told him, 'Take four birds. Tame them and teach them to always fly back to you. Then kill them and cut them into pieces. Go out to the hills, put pieces of the birds on every hill and then call them back to you. Just wait and see. They will quickly come flying back to you.'

Ibraheem did what he was told. And he saw the birds all come flying back to him. In this same way people will all quickly return to Allah when He calls them back to life after their death.

And Allah said, 'That is how life is given to the dead. And now you know how great is Allah's power and wisdom.'

Prayer for a son

Some time after he and his wife had settled in the new land, Ibraheem prayed, 'Oh my God! I do not have any children. Give me a good son.'

Allah heard Ibraheem's prayer. Ibraheem had good news that he would have a righteous son. And then the prayer was answered. Ibraheem was given a son. His name was Ismaeel.

When Ismaeel was still very small, Allah told Ibraheem to take Ismaeel and his mother Hajar to another place.

They prepared for a journey and then travelled a long way into the desert to a place called Makkah. There, near two little hills called Safa and Marwa, they stopped. This was the place where Allah told Ibraheem to leave Ismaeel and Hajar. Ibraheem listened and obeyed Allah's command. He trusted that Allah would take care of Hajar and Ismaeel. So he left them there.

Prayer for water

It was very hot and dry in the desert. Little Ismaeel was very thirsty. Hajar had to leave Ismaeel to look for water. She ran back and forth between the two hills but saw nothing to drink. How could they live without water?

Hajar prayed for water. Ismaeel would soon die if he didn't have any water to drink.

Then, to her great relief, she saw water coming out of the ground near Ismaeel. Her prayer was answered! Then she and Ismaeel could drink. How cool it was! How good it tasted!

The well of Zamzam

The water kept on coming out of the ground. There was so much water that Hajar cried out, 'Zamzam!', which meant 'Stop! Stop!'

But the cool, clear water didn't stop. It was a gushing spring of water.

Hajar and Ismaeel stayed there. The well at this spring of water was named Zamzam, after the word used by Hajar.

Other people travelling through the desert came to drink at the well of Zamzam. It never stopped flowing.

Some of the people decided to live there, too, and the place became a little town. The town was called Makkah.

Ibraheem's dream

A few years later, Ibraheem came to see Ismaeel and Hajar in Makkah.

He prayed to Allah about Makkah, saying, 'Oh my God! Make this a city of peace, and reward its people. Feed its people, the ones who believe in You, with fruits.'

One night, Ibraheem had a dream about Ismaeel. The dream upset him, and he couldn't stop thinking about it. He knew that Allah was telling him something.

Then finally, Ibraheem decided to talk to Ismaeel about his dream. He said, 'Oh, my son! I saw in a dream that I should offer you in sacrifice. It would be a very difficult thing for me to do. What do you think of this whole thing?'

The test

Now during that time, other people in the land would sometimes sacrifice a boy or girl to their gods. They had the idea that the gods wanted them to do such things, so they would kill the boy or girl as part of their worship.

Ibraheem loved his son very much. How could he sacrifice his own son? And Ismaeel did not understand why Allah would give such a command. But Ismaeel knew one thing—his father trusted Allah completely.

So Ismaeel said to his father, 'Oh my father! Do as you are told. You will find me, Insha'Allah, as someone who has patience and a strong heart.'

So both father and son, who loved each other dearly, agreed to listen to Allah. They went to a place in the desert called Mina where they could make the sacrifice.

At Mina, the father laid his son down and had the knife ready to make the sacrifice. He said, '*Allaho Akbar. Bismillah-ir-Rahman-ir-Raheem.*'

Suddenly a voice called, 'Oh Ibraheem! Stop! You have showed that you will obey Allah. This is enough. You have already fulfilled Allah's will.'

With relief, Ibraheem put down the knife. What good news! Ismaeel was saved and Ibraheem now understood that Allah had been testing him. They both thanked Allah and then sacrificed an animal that was sent by Allah.

Allah had put Ibraheem to a test to see if he would really obey him. Ibraheem passed the test, and ever after that, when people remembered how strong Prophet Ibraheem's faith in Allah had been, they have said these words: 'Peace be upon Ibraheem'.

The House of Allah

Allah told Ibraheem and Ismaeel to build a place to worship Him in Makkah.

So together, with their own hands, Ibraheem and Ismaeel made a simple building from the rocks in the desert to be the House of Allah. It was called Ka'bah.

This was the prayer that Ibraheem and Ismaeel made as they worked:

'Our God! Accept our work, for You can hear everything and know everything.

Our God! Make us people who follow Your will,

And make our children people who follow Your will;

Show us how to worship You;

And send among the people after us a prophet who will teach them about You,

For You are the Greatest and Wisest.

Watch over us with care,

For You are most Merciful.'

Pilgrimage to the House of Allah

Allah gave Ibraheem and Ismaeel special instructions.

'Worship only Me, and purify my House for the people who come here to worship.'

'The Ka'ba will be a place where everyone is safe.'

'Tell the people to come on a pilgrimage here to this sacred House. They will come on foot and with many different kinds of animals from far away places.'

'Here they will worship—they will pray and they will offer a sacrifice of animals. When they make a sacrifice, they will do it in the name of Allah, saying

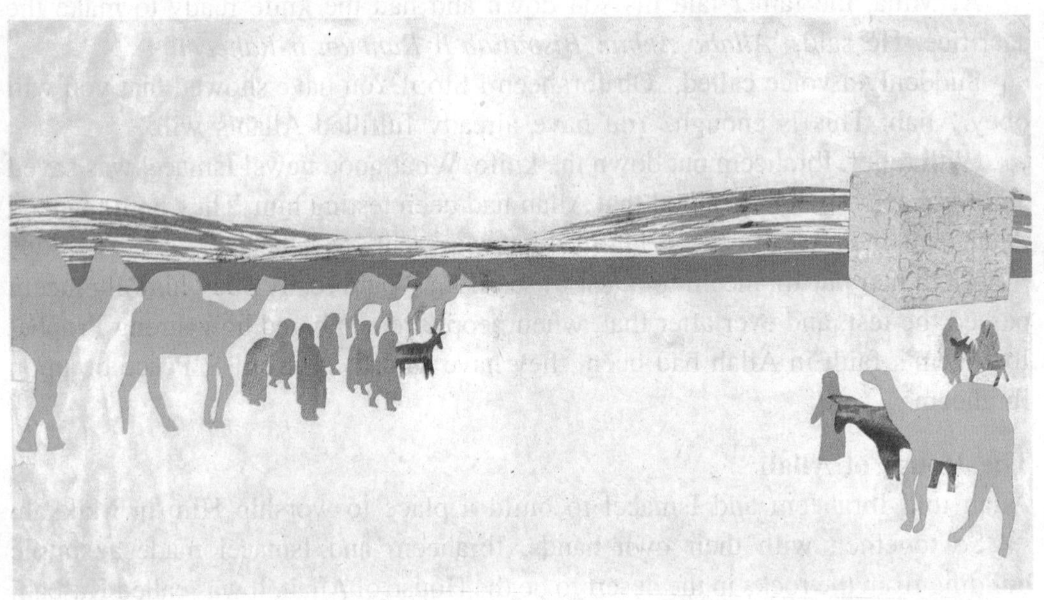

Allaho-Akbar. Then they will eat some of the meat and give the rest to people who are poor. After that they will finish their pilgrimage to the House of Allah.'

Each year since that time, people have made pilgrimage to the Ka'bah in Makkah and worship Allah in a special way. This pilgrimage is called the Hajj. During the Hajj the pilgrims remember the sacrifice of Ibraheem when they sacrifice the animals.

Whoever goes to the Ka'bah remembers this story of how it was built by Ibraheem and his son Ismaeel. May Allah's peace and blessings be on them both. At the same time, Muslims all over the world also remember the sacrifice of Ibraheem. They sacrifice animals with the words '*Allaho-Akbar. Bismillah-ir-Rahman-ir-Raheem*'. This special time is called 'Eid al-Adha.'

Messages from Allah

Ibraheem then returned to the land of Palestine where he lived with the rest of his family.

Over the years, Allah had sent Ibraheem different messages and they were put together in a book. This Book of Ibraheem then helped other people to also learn about Allah's message.

His nephew Lut, who had also moved here with his family many years ago, was sent with a message from Allah to warn the people of the towns called Sodom and Gomorrah. He lived among them and with his example and his words was trying to tell them to stop doing the bad things they did and to worship Allah.

Messengers from Allah

Many years later, some messengers from Allah came to Ibraheem. They said to him, 'Assalam-O-Alaikum!'

Ibraheem answered, 'Wa Alaikum-us-Salam!'

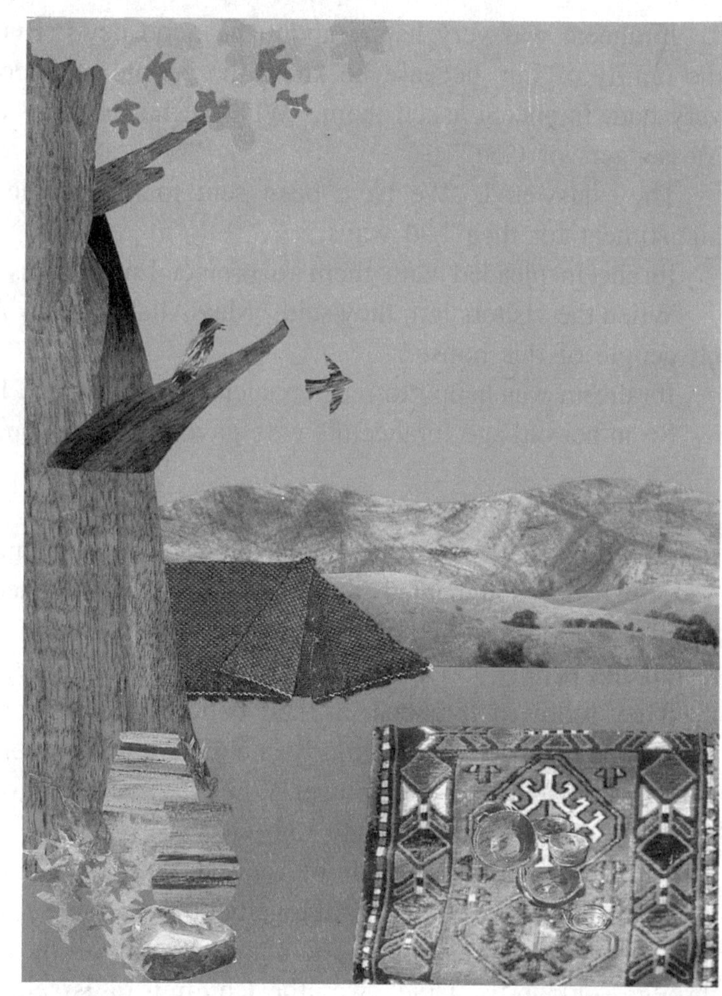

Ibraheem thought that the travellers would be hungry, so he quickly brought food for them to eat. He set a meal of roast calf in front of them and said, 'Won't you eat?' But the visitors did not reach for the food. They ate nothing.

Ibraheem thought his visitors were unusual guests and felt afraid of them. And he told them, 'We are afraid of you.'

But the visitors said, 'Do not be afraid. We have been sent by Allah to go to the people of Lut. But we also have a message for you. We bring you good news. You and your wife will have a son. He will become a wise man. His name will be Ishaq.'

Now when Ibraheem's wife heard this news about a baby she started to laugh and said, 'I am an old woman! Shall I have a child, now that I am an old woman and my husband here is an old man? That would really be a strange thing.'

The visitors said, 'Do you wonder about Allah's command? That is what Allah has said—He is full of Wisdom and Knowledge. And through Ishaq you will have a grandson Yaqoob. They will both be given knowledge by Allah and they will become leaders of the people.'

Ibraheem was very happy about the good news. But he was also afraid for the family of Lut, because he knew the people of Sodom and Gomorrah were very bad. Ibraheem asked them, 'What is the business you have to do now, oh Messengers of God?'

They answered, 'We have been sent to the people of Lut, to bring them punishment for their bad ways.'

Ibraheem pleaded with them to protect Lut and his family.

When the visitors left, they said, 'May Allah's mercy and blessings be on you, oh people of this house.'

Ibraheem was happy to receive such good news and he was no longer afraid.

So in her old age Ibraheem's wife gave birth to a son. They called him Ishaq.

A family of Prophets

In time, Ibraheem's son Ishaq had a son, too, whose name was Yaqoob. And later Yaqoob had a son named Yusuf. All of them—Ibraheem, Ishaq, Yaqoob and Yusuf—were leaders among their people. Allah chose them to be His messengers, to tell the people about the Hereafter. All of them were called prophets.

They followed Ibraheem in their belief in Allah. For them, it was important to do good deeds, to pray regularly and to give to the poor. Allah filled their hearts with wisdom and gave them power. When they were put to a test, they were faithful to Allah, and worshipped only one God.

Yusuf was not the only son of Yaqoob. He had eleven other sons, who in their turn had many more children. All together they became a very large family. Another name for Yaqoob was Israel. The name given to all the descendents of Ibraheem through Yaqoob, or Israel, was the Children of Israel.

As the years passed, the Children of Israel kept alive the belief in One God while everyone else in the world worshipped idols. Allah guided the Children of Israel and gave them His Law, the Torah, through Prophet Musa. And in later times Allah sent Prophet Isa to the Children of Israel.

Ibraheem's first son, Ismaeel, had many descendents, too. Among them came the greatest of all the prophets—Muhammad, may Allah's peace and blessings be on him.

Very early in his life, Allah had given Ibraheem this promise: 'I will make you a leader of the nations.'

When Ibraheem was an old man, he said, 'Praise be to Allah, who has given me, in my old age, Ismaeel and Ishaq. My God has really answered my prayers.'

This story about Prophet Ibraheem and his sons is found in the Noble Qur'an in different Surahs:

2:124-29,258,260;	11:69-73;	21:51-72;	38:45-77;
5:100;	15:51-56;	26:70-104;	51:24-30;
6:74-82;	19:41-49;	37:83-113;	87:19.

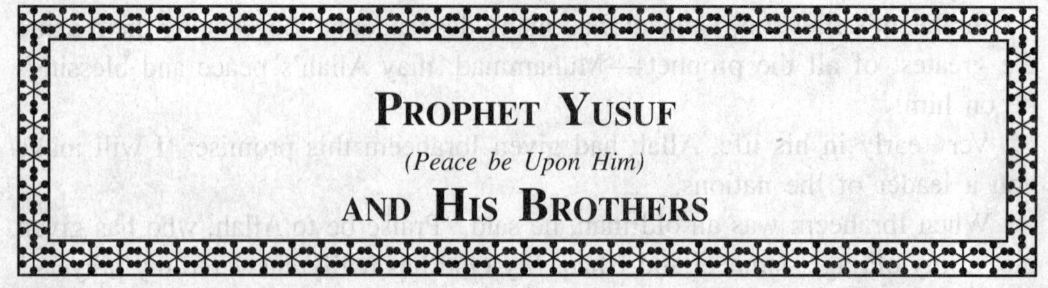

PROPHET YUSUF
(Peace be Upon Him)
AND HIS BROTHERS

The great grandson of Prophet Ibraheem

Many years after Prophet Ibraheem had left his home in Ur of the Chaldees to settle in the land where Allah wanted him to live, a very special boy was born in his family. It was his great grandson. The boy's name was Yusuf. The father of Yusuf was Yaqoob. Yaqoob's father was Ishaq. And Ishaq's father was Ibraheem. All of them had worshipped Allah and taught their children about Allah. So Yusuf, too, grew up learning about Allah.

Yusuf was a handsome boy. He was strong, too. His father, Yaqoob, loved him very much. Yusuf had eleven brothers. Sometimes they were jealous of him. They thought that their father loved Yusuf more than the others.

Yaqoob had many flocks of sheep and goats. His sons took care of the animals, moving the flocks from place to place for food. Sometimes they had to go far out in the hills to find good grass for the sheep and goats to eat. They also had to make sure that there was always enough water for the animals to drink.

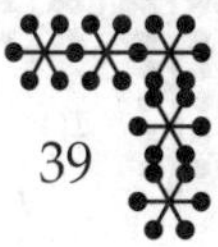

Yusuf's dream

One night Yusuf had a strange dream. In his dream he saw eleven stars and the sun and the moon. They were all there before him in the sky. The stars, the sun and the moon bowed down to him. Yusuf kept thinking about the dream and wondered what it meant. He asked his father about it.

Yaqoob understood right away that Allah was teaching Yusuf in a special way. He told his son not to tell his brothers about this dream, because they would not understand it. They might even try to hurt him. Yaqoob knew that Allah had a special plan for Yusuf.

A problem in the family

There were twelve brothers in the family and they didn't all get along with each other. The ten oldest brothers didn't like the other two. They said, 'Our father really loves Yusuf and our youngest brother more than us. But our father is old and wandering in his mind.'

They made a plan. 'We will kill Yusuf, or send him away to some unknown land. Then our father will give us everything. After that, we'll live better lives.'

But one of the brothers said, 'Do not kill Yusuf. If you have to do something, put him in the bottom of a well, and then some caravan of travellers will find him and take him away.'

The brothers went to speak to their father. 'Oh, our father! Let Yusuf come with us tomorrow when we go out to the hills with the flocks. He can play and have fun there. We'll take good care of him.'

Their father didn't like the idea. He said, 'What if a wolf will come and hurt Yusuf, and you won't help him? You know how much I love Yusuf. It will make me very sad if you take him away from me.'

The brothers said, 'If there are so many of us and a wolf kills Yusuf, then we will have been killed first.'

So they went the next day.

Bad brothers

The brothers had decided to throw Yusuf down into the bottom of a dry well. And that is what they did. Yusuf was put down there, all alone. But Yusuf was not afraid. He knew that God was with him.

The brothers went home late that night. They were crying. They said to their father, 'We were racing with each other and Yusuf stayed with the sheep. A wolf came and killed Yusuf. We know you will never believe us, but we're telling you the truth.'

Then they showed their father Yusuf's shirt. It was stained with blood from some animal. Yaqoob knew it was not Yusuf's blood on the shirt.

Yaqoob said to them, 'No, you've made up a story which you think I might believe. I can't believe that.' He was very sad. 'Now we can only look to God for help.'

Trapped in a well

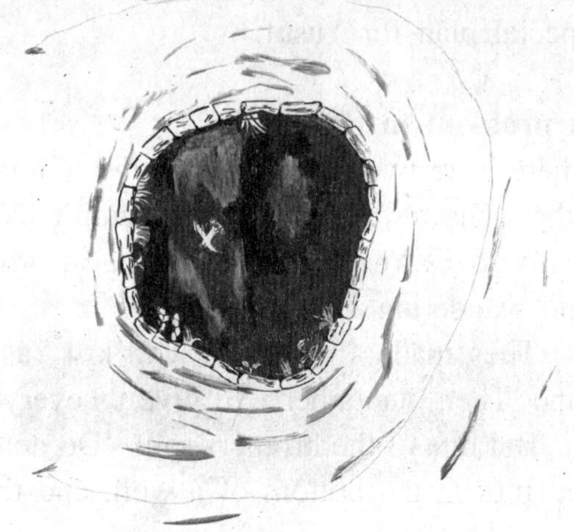

In the meanwhile, Yusuf was trapped in the bottom of the well. There was no way that he could get out by himself.

After a long time, he heard a noise above him. Someone put a bucket down into the well. It was a water carrier for a caravan of travellers. The man with the bucket was surprised to see someone in the well. He cried out to his friends, 'Oh my! Good news! Here is a beautiful young man!'

With the rope and a bucket, they brought Yusuf up out of the well. They were happy to find him and decided to hide him in the caravan and take him along. They would sell him in Egypt.

Yusuf's older brothers had been secretly watching the well where they had thrown him. They wanted to see what would happen to Yusuf. When the travellers found Yusuf, his brothers came out from their hiding place and they arranged to sell Yusuf to the men in the caravan. They sold him for a very small price.

Sold in Egypt

When the caravan of travellers moved on, Yusuf was taken with them. He was taken away from his home and family to Egypt, to a strange land far away.

After a long trip, the caravan arrived in Egypt. There Yusuf was sold to a man who was an important officer in Pharaoh's court. He was called the great Aziz.

The Aziz liked Yusuf very much. And he said to his wife, 'Treat Yusuf well. Maybe his stay here will bring us good luck, or maybe we will adopt him as our son.'

Yusuf had grown up to be a handsome man. The Aziz's wife thought Yusuf was beautiful, and she was very attracted to him. Living in the same house, she often admired him. One day she locked the doors and said to Yusuf, 'Come to me.'

Yusuf said, 'God forbid! Your husband is my master, and he has arranged for me to stay here. This is wrong. People who do such wrong things will come to no good end.'

But she wanted him. She wanted him with passion and the doors were locked. He would have given in, if he had not remembered Allah. He didn't give in to her, and they both rushed to the door. She grabbed his shirt at the back and it tore. And then, who should appear at the door but her husband.

The woman quickly said to her husband, 'What should the punishment be for a person who had an evil plan against your wife? Should it be prison, or something worse?'

Yusuf exclaimed, 'It was she who wanted me to come to her. '

Someone else in the household who was there suggested, 'If his tunic has been torn from the front, then she is telling the truth, and he is a liar! But if his shirt is torn from the back, then she is the liar and he is telling the truth.'

So they looked at the shirt and saw that it was torn at the back, and the Aziz said to his wife, 'Look at this! This shows how cunning you are. ' He turned to Yusuf, 'But Yusuf, let this pass.' To his wife he said, 'And my wife, ask forgiveness for your sin, for really, it was your fault.'

Now the women in the city started to talk about this with each other. They were saying, 'The wife of the great Aziz is in love with her slave-boy. Her love for him has pierced her heart. Yes, we can see she's suffering and is going astray.'

When she heard about their malicious gossip, she sent for them and prepared a luxurious feast. They came. When she handed out a knife to each of them, she called for Yusuf, 'Come out and show yourself.'

When the ladies saw him, they were amazed at his beauty. They became so flustered that they cut their hands with their knives and exclaimed, 'God save us. This can't be anything but a noble angel.'

The Aziz's wife told them, 'This, then, is the man about whom you have been blaming me. And it's true, I did try to make him come to me, but he refused.

But now, however, if he does not do what I ask him to do, he shall most certainly be imprisoned, and shall find himself among people who are despised.'

Yusuf said, 'Oh my Lord! I'd rather go to prison than do what these women want me to do. Unless you turn their cunning ways from me, I might still get caught up by them and become one of those people who are unaware of right and wrong.'

So, Allah heard his prayer and turned the women's snare away from Yusuf. After Aziz and his household saw what had happened, even after they had seen all the signs that Yusuf was innocent, they decided that it was best to put Yusuf out of sight for a while, so he was put in prison.

While in prison, Yusuf had a lot of time to think about his life, about what his father had taught him, about Allah. He knew that Allah was watching over him.

And while he was in prison, two men who worked for the Pharaoh were also sent there. They had some dreams which they couldn't understand and they told Yusuf about their dreams.

The first one, who had been the Pharaoh's cupbearer—the man who brought the Pharaoh whatever he wanted to drink—said, 'I saw myself in a dream, pressing grapes.'

The second one, who had been the Pharaoh's baker, said, 'I saw myself in a dream carrying bread on my head, and the birds were eating it.'

They said to Yusuf, 'We can see that you are a good man. Tell us the meaning of our dreams.'

Yusuf said to them, 'I will soon tell you what they mean. You'll know the meanings before our next meal. But first, let me tell you about something that is very important.'

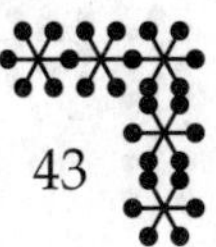

Believe in one God

Yusuf had seen how people in Egypt worshipped things other than Allah. They talked about the god of the earth, the god of the sea, the god of the crops and the god of the rain. He wanted to tell people to worship the one true God.

So then Yusuf talked to the prisoners about believing in Allah. 'There are people who don't believe in Allah or even in life after death. I follow the ways of my fathers—Ibraheem, Ishaq and Yaqoob—and we believe there is only one God.'

'You are my friends here in prison. I'll ask you a question: Is it better to believe in many different kinds of gods or Allah who is God of everything? Look at the earth and the heavens and everything in it. This is the creation of Allah. Just show me what those other gods have created. If you don't believe in One God, you only have some kind of ideas that you and your fathers have come up with. We should worship only the One God. Most people don't understand this, but this is the right way to believe.'

And then Yusuf talked to them about their dreams. For the one man, he had good news. For the other, he had bad news. He said, 'My two friends here in prison—one of you will go back to pour the wine for the Pharaoh to drink. The other will hang from a cross, and the birds will eat from his head. This is the meaning of what you asked me.'

Yusuf then turned to the man who was going to be set free from prison and said, 'Speak to the Pharaoh about me.'

What Yusuf told the men came true. One man was sentenced to death and the other one went back to work for the Pharaoh. But the man who was set free forgot to tell the Pharaoh about Yusuf and so Yusuf had to stay in prison some more years.

The Pharaoh's dream

One night the Pharaoh of Egypt had a dream. He saw that there were seven fat cows and seven thin cows. The seven thin cows ate the fat ones. Then he saw that there were seven green cobs of corn and also seven other corn cobs, all dry and withered.

The Pharaoh asked many men to help him understand his dream. But no one could tell him the meaning of his dream. They said, 'What a mixed-up dream! We don't know what it could mean.'

Then the man who had once been in prison with Yusuf remembered how Yusuf had helped him and his friend understand their dreams. The man said to the Pharaoh, 'I can find out the meaning of your dream! I will be back soon.'

The man went straight to the prison to talk to Yusuf. He said, 'You are a man who tells the truth. What does this dream mean? Seven fat cows are eaten by seven thin cows, and there are seven green cobs of corn and seven others that are all dry and withered. Tell me what it means, so that I can go back to the people and they will understand.'

Yusuf explained, 'For seven years, farmers should work hard, and the crops will be very good. Some food could be eaten but the rest should be put away safely. After that there will be dry years when there will be no crops, and very little food, and people will be hungry. Some grain should be kept in a special place to be used for seed. It should not be eaten, because after the seven dry years are over, there will be a time when the crops will grow. Then there will be lots of water again, and people will make wine and oil.'

The man hurried back to the Pharaoh with the meaning of his dream.

From prison to palace

When the Pharaoh heard the meaning of his dream, he wanted to see who had understood it. He asked a messenger to go get Yusuf from the prison and bring him to the palace.

But when the Pharaoh's messenger came to Yusuf in the prison, Yusuf said to him, 'Go back to the Pharaoh and ask him this question: "What is in the minds of the people who caused me to be sent to prison in the first place?" If the Pharaoh doesn't know why I was sent here, certainly my God knows what was happening.'

So the messenger went back to the Pharaoh and everything was investigated. It was proven that Yusuf had not done anything wrong. The Pharaoh said, 'Bring Yusuf to me. He will become my special helper.'

Yusuf was brought to the Pharaoh. Finally he was out of that terrible prison.

The Pharaoh was thankful to Yusuf for having understood the dream. And he said, 'Now we all know that you are an honest man. From now on, you will be an important officer in my court.'

Yusuf said, 'Make me in charge of the storehouses of the land, to supervise the harvest of the crops and to make sure the grain is in safe storage.'

So Yusuf became an important man in the Pharaoh's court. He prepared the whole country for seven dry years, when people would be hungry and need food. He worked hard to help the people of Egypt. But all the time, he kept thinking about his home far away, about his family and especially about his father. He was longing to see his father and his younger brother, whom he loved very much.

A trip to buy corn

Far away in Yusuf's childhood home, his father and the rest of his family were hungry. They didn't have very much to eat. When the brothers heard that there was grain in Egypt, they went there to buy food.

When the brothers came to Egypt to buy grain, Yusuf saw them and sold them grain. He asked them many questions: 'Do you have a father at home? Is he old? Was this too far for him to travel? Do you have other brothers? . ..' The brothers did not know that this was Yusuf. They thought he was a great Egyptian.

Yusuf said to them, 'Come again. You have seen that you get your money's worth of corn, and that you are well taken care of while you are here. The next time you come, you must bring your brother along. If you do not bring him to me, I will not sell you any more corn. Then I will not even speak with you.'

The brothers answered, 'We will certainly try to tell our father this . . . Yes, we will do it.'

And Yusuf did something else. He told the men who packed the saddle bags for his brothers to put the money they had paid for the corn back in their bags. This was to make sure that they would return soon.

A surprise in the saddle bags

The brothers made the long trip home. When they returned they said to their father right away, 'Oh our father! We won't be able to buy any more grain in Egypt unless we take Ben Yamin along. So send him with us, and we will take very good care of him.'

Yaqoob answered, 'Should I trust you with your youngest brother any more than I trusted you with his brother before?'

Then they opened their bags to look at the grain, and were surprised to find that their money was in the bags, too. They said to their father, 'What more could we want? Our money was given back to us! Now we can go back to Egypt and get more food. We'll take good care of our brother and add a camel's load of grain to what we already have. This isn't much that we have.'

Yaqoob said, 'I will never ever send him with you until you make a promise to me, in the name of Allah, that unless you yourselves are caught and trapped, you will be sure to bring him back to me.'

The brothers made their promise.

Then Yaqoob said, 'Allah has seen and heard everything that we have just said.'

Then he also gave his sons some advice: 'My sons! When you get to Egypt, do not all go into the city through one gate. Go in through different gates. And remember to trust in Allah.'

A second trip to buy corn

So the eleven brothers travelled to Egypt and went into the city the way their father had asked them to go. They went to see Yusuf. Yusuf was very happy to see them, especially his youngest brother. The brothers still did not know that this man in Egypt was their own brother. But Yusuf took Ben Yamin to his side, and said, 'Look! I am your own brother. Don't be sad about everything they're doing.' He talked with Ben Yamin a lot. The two good brothers were finally together.

The Pharaoh's cup

Yusuf wanted to have his father Yaqoob and his whole family come live with him in Egypt. How could he do it? He made a plan. After the saddle bags were packed with the grain the brothers had bought, Yusuf secretly hid a special drinking cup in Ben Yamin's bag. Then the brothers left for home.

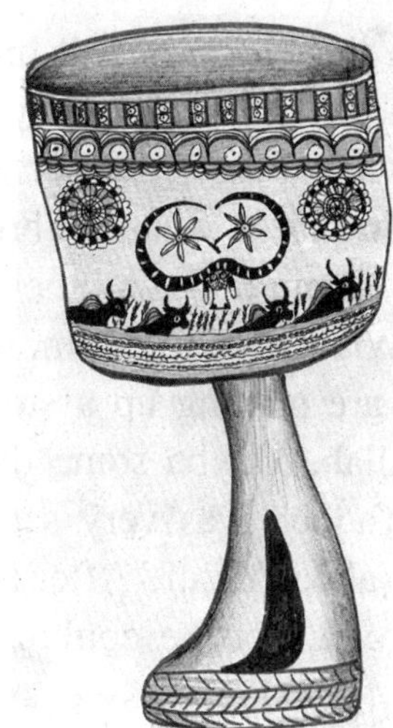

As they were travelling out across the desert, they heard someone shouting at them. 'Stop! Stop the caravan! You are thieves!'

The brothers stopped their animals and saw the guards from the Pharaoh of Egypt's court. They said, 'What's wrong?'

The guards said, 'The best drinking cup of the Pharaoh is missing. There is a great reward for whoever finds it—as much as a camel can carry. Where is the cup?'

The brothers said, 'We are not thieves. We came to Egypt to buy food, not to steal things. You know that.'

The Egyptian guards asked the brothers, 'What if what you say is not true? What if we find the cup with you, then what shall be done?'

The brothers said, 'The person who has the cup will be taken. That person will not be free.'

So all the saddle bags were searched. The guards looked everywhere. Where was the king's cup? Finally it was found. It was in Ben Yamin's bag. They all went back to the Pharaoh's court.

Bad news

The brothers were puzzled that the cup was found in Ben Yamin's bag. Then they said, 'If he steals, we remember his other brother, who also stole things.'

Yusuf heard them say this, and knew it was not true, and still he did not tell the ten brothers who he was. He said to himself, 'You are all in a bad way, and Allah knows what is really true.'

The brothers cried to Yusuf, 'Please, please let him return to his old father, who will be very sad if our brother does not go home. Take one of us instead. You are a good man. Let Ben Yamin be free.'

But Yusuf said, 'No. We must take the one who had the cup. It would be wrong to take someone else.' None of their pleading would change Yusuf's mind.

The brothers then had a meeting by themselves. One of the brothers said, 'Can't you remember the promise we made to our father? And remember how we didn't take care of Yusuf? I will not leave Egypt until my father tells me to leave. Now you go back to our father and tell him what happened. Tell him Ben Yamin stole from the Pharaoh. Tell him we couldn't do anything about it. Tell him to ask in the town where we were and to ask the other people in the caravan. And then he will know it is true.'

So that is what the brothers did. One of them stayed in Egypt, to watch over Ben Yamin and the other nine brothers went home to tell Yaqoob the bad news.

When they told him, their father did not believe what they said. He said, 'No. You are making up a story again. I do not believe you. I will wait, and I trust in Allah. Maybe some day Allah will bring us all together again.'

Yaqoob was very sad. He turned away from his sons and cried, 'How sad I am about Yusuf.' After that, Yaqoob was sick with sadness. His eyesight became blurred. Then he couldn't see. And then he stopped talking.

Many days passed and the brothers were not kind to their old father. They said to Yaqoob, 'By Allah! Will you never stop thinking about Yusuf? You make yourself sick and you'll die just thinking about him.'

Yaqoob said to them, 'I only complain about my distress and lack of patience to Allah. I know that Allah takes care of us. Now my sons, go and ask about Yusuf and his brother in Egypt. I believe Allah is taking care of them both. Only people who do not believe in Allah have no hope.'

A third trip to Egypt

The brothers went to Egypt, and went back to see Yusuf and tell him about their problems. They told him, 'We have great sadness in our family. And now we have only a little money to buy grain. Give us more, please, because our family at home is hungry. We know you are a good man.'

Then Yusuf asked, 'Do you remember what you did to Yusuf? And to his brother? Do you remember how you treated them?'

The brothers were surprised to be asked such questions. This man knew everything about them! Then it was their turn to ask him who he was. Perhaps, just perhaps, could this powerful man in Egypt be the brother they had sold to a caravan years and years ago?

'Are you Yusuf?' the brothers asked.

'Yes, I am Yusuf' And pointing to Ben Yamin, he said, 'And this is my brother. Allah has taken care of us all. Allah takes care of everyone who does what is right.'

The brothers were still surprised and said, 'Allah has really taken care of you. We did wrong things. What we did to you was bad.'

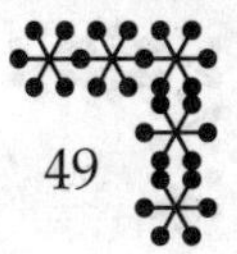

Yusuf said, 'From now on, let us be friends. Allah will forgive you. Now take my shirt to my father, and put it over his face. He will know that it is mine. Then he will see clearly and he will understand. All of you must come to Egypt, with your families, to live here with me.'

Good news for Yaqoob

When the brothers left Egypt in a caravan to go back home with the good news about Yusuf, their father at home knew that something was happening. He could feel in the air something about Yusuf. Even before the caravan arrived, Yaqoob knew, and he told others around him. They thought he was old and crazy. But he said to them, 'Don't think I am saying this because I'm old.'

When the brothers finally got home, they gave their father Yusuf's shirt and put it over his eyes. Yaqoob's eyes became clear and he could see again. Then Yaqoob said to his sons, 'Didn't I tell you that I know from Allah what you do not know?'

The sons said, 'Yes, our father, we were wrong, and we are sorry. Ask Allah to forgive us for what we did wrong.'

Yaqoob said, 'I will ask Allah to forgive you. He is all forgiving and merciful.' Yaqoob was filled with happiness.

Together at last

The whole family, Yusuf's parents and his brothers and their wives and children, all moved to Egypt. When they got there, they all went to see Yusuf. They bowed down on the ground in front of him.

Yusuf said to his father, 'Oh my! This is my dream from long, long ago. Allah has made it come true!'

Yusuf gave them all places to live. Yaqoob and his mother lived with Yusuf in his home.

Here in Egypt there was plenty of food for everyone. And now finally, the whole family was together again.

Yusuf was very thankful, and said to his father, ' Allah has been good to me. He took me out of prison and brought all of you here out of the desert. This was

even after my brothers and I had become enemies. Allah has a plan, and Allah understands all things.'

And Yusuf prayed to Allah: 'Oh my God! You have really given me some power and taught me something about the meaning of dreams and things that happen in the world. You are the Maker of the heavens and the earth. You are my Protector in this world and the next. Take my soul to You when I die, and put me with those who have been on the right path.'

This story about Prophet Yusuf is found in the Noble Qur'an in this Surah.
12:1-101.

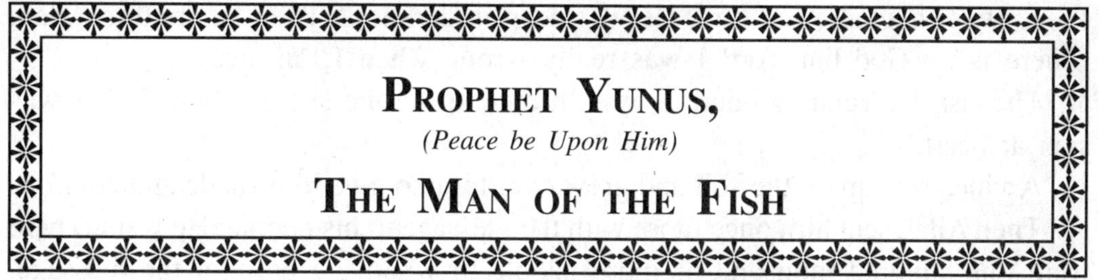

Prophet Yunus,

(Peace be Upon Him)

The Man of the Fish

Prophet Yunus was sent with a message to his people. But they didn't want to listen to him and wouldn't accept his message. So Yunus ran away in great anger. He ran like a slave who had escaped and he thought Allah had no power over him.

Yunus got away on to a ship that was fully loaded and ready to sail. When the ship was out at sea, it was caught in a bad storm. The sailors had a superstition, that someone on board caused the bad weather, so they cast lots and the lot fell on Yunus. He was then thrown overboard.

A big fish swallowed him. He was deep in darkness. Then he cried to Allah, 'There is no God but You! I was really wrong when I ran away.'

The fish let Yunus go and he was thrown up on the shore. There Yunus was sick at heart.

A vine grew up on the soil and grew over him, to give him shade and comfort.

Then Allah sent him once more with the message to his people. He went. There were one hundred thousand or more people to whom he brought the message. This time people believed him and his message. Allah allowed Yunus' people to enjoy their life for a while longer.

If Yunus had not been a person who, from even in the deep darkness of distress, could see Allah's glory, he would have stayed in the belly of the fish till the Day when everyone will be raised from the dead. But Yunus praised God. He had run away from the city, been thrown overboard from the ship, and he had been swallowed by a sea animal. After all this, he still praised Allah. And Allah listened to him. Because he was faithful to God, Allah helped him out of his trouble.

Yunus was known as Zun-nun, which means 'the man of the fish.'

Even though Yunus had been impatient and tried to get away, Allah brought him back and he was made to be in the company of the righteous.

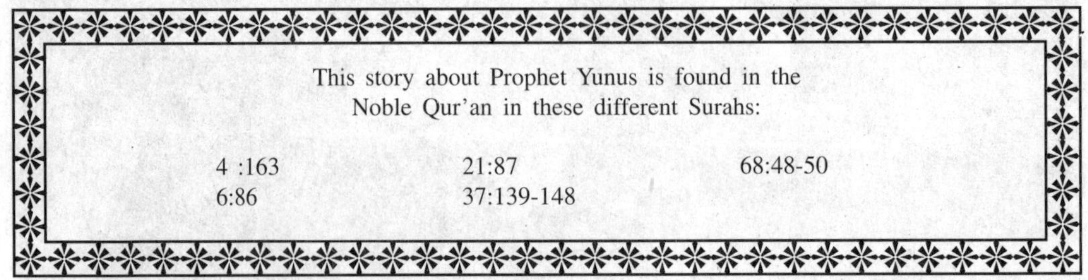

This story about Prophet Yunus is found in the Noble Qur'an in these different Surahs:

4 :163	21:87	68:48-50
6:86	37:139-148	

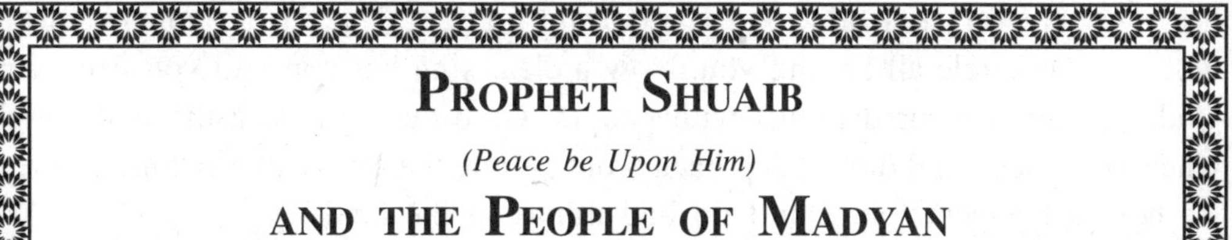

PROPHET SHUAIB

(Peace be Upon Him)

AND THE PEOPLE OF MADYAN

A message for the people of Madyan

The Madyan people were a wandering tribe that lived in the lands of Arabia. These nomads were also called the People of the Thicket. They lived on the trade routes that went between Egypt and Mesopotamia so they had business dealings with the many caravans that crossed their territory. Many of the Madyan traders were very shrewd. A lot of their trading was not done honestly. And so the Madyans became a large and powerful tribe, with innumerable flocks of sheep and goats and herds of camels.

Allah chose a man from the Madyan tribe to be a messenger to his own people. His name was Shuaib, which means 'one whose heart is on fire with Allah's love'.

Shuaib said, 'Oh my people! Worship Allah. You have no other god but Him.

I see you are very rich now, but I am afraid for you. There is a punishment that will one day circle all around you. Now a clear sign has come to you from your God. Be fair in your dealings with people. Give the right measure and weight when you trade. And don't keep back from people the things that belong to them. Be honest businessmen. Don't do bad things in the land.'

'What Allah gives you honestly is best for you. If only you believed! But I am not set over you to keep watch.'

'Do not squat on every road and threaten others, making it hard for those who believe in Allah to live in the right way. Don't go looking for something bad and crooked everywhere. Remember how all the Madyans were small and poor at one time, and how Allah has helped you. And hold in your mind's eye what happened to those people in the past who did wrong.'

The people don't believe

The people asked Shuaib for advice, 'Oh Shuaib! Does your worship of Allah command you that we should stop the worship which our fathers practised, or that we should stop doing what we like with our property? Really, you are the one who knows what is right!'

Shuaib said, 'Oh my people! You can see whether or not I have a clear sign from my God. He has given me strength and helped me, as if from Himself. I do not want to do the very things which I tell you not to do. I only want, to the best of my power, to help you. My success in this can only come from Allah. I trust Him and look to Him.'

Shuaib tried to explain. 'Oh my people! You know that I am not like you. But that doesn't mean that I don't feel for you. Don't let this make you to do wrong things. Don't let yourselves suffer the same terrible end as the people of Nuh or of Hud or of Saleh. And the people of Lut are not far from you. But ask forgiveness from Allah and change your ways. For my God is really full of love and kindness.'

They said, 'Oh Shuaib! We do not really understand what you say. In fact, we see that among us you have no strength. If it weren't for your family, we would certainly have stoned you. You have no power or influence among us.'

He said to them, 'Oh my people! Does my family count more with you than Allah? You throw Him away behind your backs with anger. But really, my God knows everything that you do.'

They said, 'You are speaking nonsense! You are no more than a man just like us. And we think you are a liar!'

'There is a group among you who believes in the message with which I have been sent, and a group which does not believe. Just wait and have patience. Allah will decide between us. He is the best judge.'

The leaders of the Madyans were proud people, and said, 'Oh Shuaib! We shall certainly drive you out of our city—you and those who believe with you. Or else you and they should be like us again. Change back to our ways and our religion.'

Shuaib said, 'What?!! Even though we detest them? We would really be making up a lie against Allah if we changed back to your ways after Allah had rescued us from them. And there is no way we could return to them anyway, unless it was the will and plan of Allah. Our God knows everything that is hidden. We trust Allah.'

Shuaib told them, 'Do whatever you can. I will do my part. Soon we will know who will be disgraced in the end and who is a liar. And you better watch out. I am watching, too, with you.'

The end of the people of Madyan

Shuaib spoke to Allah, 'Our God! You decide in truth between us and our people, for You are the best to decide.'

The leaders of the Madyans did not believe. To Shuaib they said, 'Now cause a piece of the sky to fall on us, if you are telling the truth!' And to their own people they said, 'If you follow Shuaib, be sure that then you are ruined.'

So Shuaib left them and said, 'Oh my people! I did bring you the message which I was sent to bring you from my God. I gave you good counsel, but how shall I cry over a people who refused to believe?

When Allah sent the command, there was a mighty blast. There was an earthquake that took them by surprise, and they lay dead in their homes before the morning. The men who had rejected Shuaib were as if they had never been in the homes where they had lived so richly before.

It was the men who rejected Shuaib who were ruined. Shuaib and those who believed with him were saved.

The story of the Prophet Shuaib is found in the following Surahs:
7:85-93 11:84-95 26:176-89 29:36-7

PROPHET MUSA

(Peace be Upon Him)

The Children of Israel in Egypt

Many, many years ago, Yusuf, the son of Yaqoob, brought his family to live with him in Egypt. Yaqoob had twelve sons and they had all moved to Egypt with their wives and children. Yaqoob's other name was Israel, and the whole family was named after him. They were called the Children of Israel.

During the time of Yusuf, the Pharaoh of Egypt had been very kind and helpful to Yusuf and his family. But the kings who came later were not good, they did not believe in Allah and they hated the Children of Israel. The kings made the Children of Israel work as slaves. The work they had to do was very very hard. They had to make bricks out of clay, straw and water. They had to cut and move huge stones. The slaves built big buildings. They built the huge pyramids where the kings were buried after they died. The slaves always had to work under the hot sun of the desert.

There was a king who came to the throne and was dazzled by his kingdom and his palaces. He said, 'Do I not own the kingdom of Egypt and these flowing rivers? I am your god!' He commanded all the people to worship him.

So while the Pharaoh of Egypt lived in his beautiful palaces beside the Nile River, the Children of Israel did not have good places to live. Their houses were small and very crowded. They did not bow down to worship the Pharaoh, and he became very angry with the Israelites.

The Pharaoh saw how many Children of Israel there were and he knew that they didn't want to be slaves for the Egyptians. He was afraid that maybe they would become more powerful than the Egyptians. He was told that a child would be born among the Israelites who would become powerful and cause the Pharaoh's kingdom to wither away. So he made a plan. The Pharaoh ordered that all baby boys born among the Israelites should be killed.

Baby in a box

There was a woman among the Children of Israel who was going to have a baby. When the baby was born and she saw that it was a boy, she was very upset. She could not let her baby be killed! So she hid her baby.

The baby's name was Musa ibn Imran, which means 'Musa, son of Imran'. As Musa grew bigger, it was hard to hide him. Allah knew what was in the mother's heart. Allah had a plan for little Musa, and gave the mother an idea. 'Keep your baby close to you. But when you are afraid that he will be discovered, put him out on the river, and let the water of the river carry him away. Do not be afraid or sad about him. He will be safe, and he will even be brought back to you.'

So the mother made a little box for her baby. She put Musa in the little box, floated it on the water of the river and pushed it out on to the Nile River. Musa's mother was very sad. But Allah made her heart strong. She said to her daughter, 'Follow him.' So the girl watched the box with her brother move down the river and followed it along the riverbank.

The box floated down the Nile River. Who should see the little box but the people from the Pharaoh's palace! Musa's sister saw how they took the little box, opened it up, and had such a surprise to find a beautiful baby inside. They could see that he was a baby from the Children of Israel. Musa's sister saw how the wife of the Pharaoh wanted to keep the baby. She heard her say to the Pharaoh, 'This is a beautiful baby. Do not kill him. He can grow up here. Maybe he can help us, or maybe we can keep him as our own son.'

Musa's sister saw there was another problem. Her little baby brother wouldn't drink milk or eat anything in that strange place. Then she had an idea, so she left the place where she was hiding, went to the the Queen, and said, 'Shall I show you someone who could feed this baby and would take good care of him?' What a good idea! So she did. Baby Musa's real mother was asked to feed him. His mother now knew Allah's promise was true and she was very thankful to Allah.

Musa grows up

Musa grew up like a prince in the Pharaoh's palace. He studied everything the Egyptians learned in school. He learned everything about the Egyptian way of life. At the same time, his mother taught him all about Allah and believing in one God.

Musa saw the rich life of the royal family and he saw the sad and miserable lives of the Israelite slaves. Every day, he felt the anger in his heart, but he didn't say anything. Allah gave him knowledge and helped him understand many things.

Musa leaves the palace

When he was a young man Musa decided one night to go out into the city. He went out from the palace at a time when no one would see him leave and he walked alone in the city streets.

On one of the streets, he saw two men fighting with each other. One was an Egyptian and the other was one of the Children of Israel. When the Israelite saw Musa—one of his own people—he called out, 'Help! Help me in this fight!' Musa was angry with the Egyptian and jumped in to get the Israelite free. He hit the Egyptian with his fist and the man fell. The Egyptian was dead. Musa felt very bad. Here he was, secretly away from the palace, taking the side of the people the king hated, and he had killed an Egyptian. Musa prayed, 'Oh my God! I have really done what was wrong. Forgive me.' Allah did forgive Musa. And Musa made a promise to Allah. 'Because you have kept me safe, I will never help people who do wrong things.'

Musa was afraid to return to the palace and wandered around in the city all night. Then it was morning. As he was walking along, he heard someone call him. There was the man whom he had helped the night before fighting again with another Egyptian. The man was calling loudly for help. Musa said to him, 'You really get into a lot of trouble.' But Musa decided to help him fight off the Egyptian.

The Egyptian looked at Musa and knew who he was and became afraid, 'Oh Musa! Do you want to kill me too, like you killed a man yesterday? You live in the palace and talk about setting things right, but you just want to push us around.'

Another man came running from the furthest end of the city. He was breathless as he told Musa, 'Oh Musa! The ministers at the palace are having a meeting about you. They plan to kill you. So go away quickly. Believe me. What I say is true.'

Musa leaves Eygpt

Musa realized that his life was in great danger. He could not go back to the palace. He could not stay in the city. He could not be anywhere where the king could find him. Musa prayed to Allah, 'Oh my God! Save me from these people.'

Musa was running for his life. He went towards the land of Madyan and said, 'I hope that Allah will show me the right way to go.'

An oasis in the desert

Musa travelled into the Madyan desert. He saw the trees of an oasis. That is where he went, where he could get water to drink and shade from the burning sun.

There were many flocks of sheep and goats at the oasis. A group of men were giving water to their animals. There were two women keeping their flocks back behind all the rest. Musa saw what was happening. He went to the women and asked, 'What is wrong? Why don't you water your flocks?' They said to him, 'We cannot water our flocks until the men take back their animals. Our father is a very old man and cannot come here to do this work. So we must wait.'

So Musa made a place at the well for their animals to drink, gave them water and then went back to the shade of the palm trees. Here he was in the middle of the desert, with no home, no work, no family, no friend. In his heart he felt very disturbed. He prayed, 'Oh my God, I really need whatever help You send me.'

While he was still sitting there, one of the young women came walking back to him. She was very shy, and said to Musa, 'My father wants to see you, so that he can thank you for having watered our flocks for us.'

Musa was happy to go, and when he met the old father he told him about everything that had happened—who he was, how he had been brought up in the palace of the Pharaoh in Egypt, how the Israelites were slaves to the Egyptians and why he had left Egypt.

The old man listened to Musa's whole story and finally said, 'Do not be afraid any longer. It is good that you have escaped from those people who live in such a bad way.'

Musa joins the family

Musa stayed with this small family for a while as their guest. The father and his daughters were happy that he had come, and they wanted him to stay. And one day one of the daughters said to her father, 'Why don't you give Musa work here with us? He is a good man. He is strong and he can be trusted.'

The old man thought about this for some time and had another idea. Then he called Musa to him and said, 'I would like for one of my daughters to marry you. You are a wanderer and have nothing you can bring to a marriage, but instead you can promise to work here for me for eight years. If you want, you can work for ten years. I will not give you any problems. You will find me, *Insha 'Allah*, a good man.'

Musa agreed to marry a daughter. He said, 'Whether I work here for eight years or for ten years, there should be no bad feelings against me. Allah knows what we have said today.'

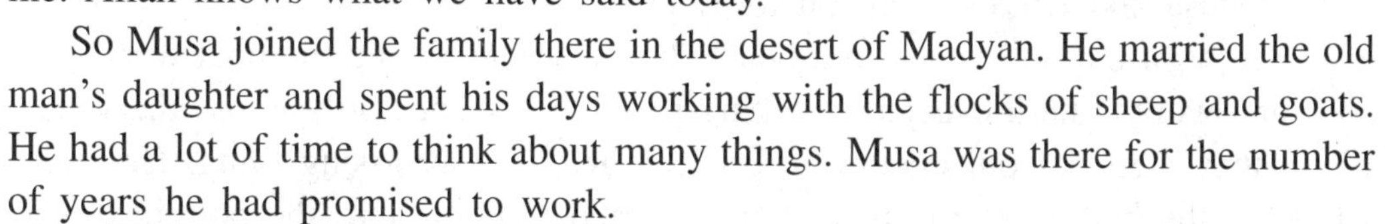

So Musa joined the family there in the desert of Madyan. He married the old man's daughter and spent his days working with the flocks of sheep and goats. He had a lot of time to think about many things. Musa was there for the number of years he had promised to work.

The test of patience

Once Musa was to go and find a special teacher who would teach him things he did not already know. He did not know exactly where he would find the teacher, but it was in a place where the two seas joined. He was to carry a fish in a basket. There would be a sign. The fish would disappear when he got to the place where he should meet this teacher.

It was hard to travel in that area of the desert, and Musa and his helper were very tired.

Musa said to his helper, 'I will not give up until I get to the place where the rivers join, or until I have been travelling for years and years.'

They travelled a long time and when they climbed a high rocky place, they saw the water where the seas joined. They were so tired when they got to this place that they had a rest and forgot about the fish.

Then they continued on, and Musa finally said, 'It is time to eat. It's been a hard trip and we are very tired. Bring the food for the meal.'

Then his helper said, 'Remember what happened when we had climbed the rock? That's where the fish disappeared. I forgot to tell you. I saw the fish. It swam in the sea in a wonderful way.'

Musa said, 'That's the place we were looking for!' So they turned around and went back on the same path they had come.

Back at the right place, they met a man. His name was Khidhr. He had been taught by Allah to know and understand many things.

Musa asked him, 'May I follow you to learn some of the special things which Allah has taught you?'

Khidhr said, 'You really wouldn't have patience with me. And how could you wait long enough to learn things which you can't understand?'

Musa said, 'You will find me, *Insha' Allah*, very patient, and I will obey whatever you say.'

The man then said, 'Alright then, but if you follow me you must not ask any questions until I talk to you about it.'

So Musa and Khidhr went on together.

They went out on the sea in a boat. The men who owned the boat were very poor and worked hard every day, taking people back and forth across the water. When they were far out on the water, Khidhr did a surprising thing. He made a hole in the bottom of the boat. Water started to come into the bottom of the boat. Musa did not understand.

Later Musa said,'Did you make the hole in the boat so that the people would drown? You did such a strange thing!'

Khidhr answered, 'Didn't I tell you that you wouldn't have patience with me?'

Musa said, 'Don't be angry with me for forgetting.'

Then they went on. They met a young man. And what did Khidhr do? He killed him.

Musa was upset. He said, 'Have you killed a man who hasn't done anything wrong? What a terrible thing you've done!'

Khidhr said, 'Didn't I tell you that you wouldn't have patience with me?'

Musa felt bad. He said, 'If I ever ask you about anything more after this, you can go on without me. Then I will not have any more excuses.'

So they went on again. They came to a town. They were both hungry and went in to the town, but no one gave them anything to eat. They asked people for some food but no one would give them any.

As Musa and Khidhr walked in the streets, they saw a wall that was just about to fall down. Khidhr found some rocks and worked on the wall, setting it straight again. When he was finished, they went on their way.

Musa said to Khidhr, 'If you had wanted, you really could have asked for something to pay for your work.'

Then Khidhr turned to Musa and said, 'This is where you and I go on our own ways. But first I will tell you why I did those things which you couldn't understand.'

Khidhr explained,

'The boat belonged to very poor men. There was a king there who was after them. He was taking all the good boats away from boatmen. If the king had taken their boat, they would have had nothing. I just wanted to make a hole in it so they couldn't use their boat. This way, after the danger was past, they could just fix it again and keep on with their work.'

'The young man had done many bad things, and would keep on doing them. It was hard for his parents, because they were good people and he was working against them and against Allah. The son would have brought them more sadness with his terrible way of life. So I killed him; and Allah promised the parents another son who would be better. The new son would love his parents.'

'The wall in the town was going to fall over. This wall had been given to two young children by their father, who was a good man. The secret was that their father had buried a treasure underneath that wall for the children. If the wall had fallen down, the people in the town would have taken the treasure away from the children. Remember how they treated us? Allah wanted the children to grow up and get the treasure for themselves.'

'So that is why I did those things. I didn't do them on my own. It was Allah's will. This is the meaning of those things which you could not understand.'

And then Musa knew it was time to move on.

Musa on the mountain

Musa was travelling in the desert with his small family. He looked up towards Mount Toor and thought he saw some smoke on the mountain. He said to his family, 'wait here. I see a fire on the mountain. I will go and check to see what is there.'

Musa climbed the mountain. When he came to the fire, he heard a voice coming from the slope, from near a tree. 'Oh, Musa! Take off your shoes. You are in the sacred valley of Tuwa.' Musa was frightened. He took off his shoes.

'I am Allah, the God of the Worlds. I have chosen you. Listen carefully to what I have to tell you.'

'There is no other god, so worship only Me. Pray regularly to remember this. The time is coming when people will be judged for how they have lived. When exactly this will happen is hidden, but don't let the people who do bad things and live wickedly fool you. Don't you follow them.'

The voice said, 'What is that in your right hand, Musa?'

Musa answered, 'It is my walking stick. I lean on it when I walk. I beat down leaves with it for my flocks. I use it for many other things, too.'

The voice said, 'Musa, throw your stick down.'

Musa threw down his stick and look! . . . It was a snake, slithering along on the ground. Musa jumped back, afraid.

The voice said, 'Oh Musa! Do not be afraid. Take it and it will turn back into your walking stick.'

And that is what happened.

'Now put your hand near your heart, and see, it becomes bright and shining.' When Musa looked at his hand, he saw that it really was shining. 'Keep your hand close to your side, to protect you from being afraid. Allah gives you these two signs. Now go to the Pharaoh of Egypt. He and his people have gone too far in their wickedness. You must speak with him.'

Musa said, 'Oh my God—I am afraid he will kill me. I killed a man in Egypt.'

The voice said, 'Musa, you are safe.'

Musa said, 'Oh my God—I cannot speak well. My brother, Haroon can speak better than I. Send him with me as my helper, to make me strong.'

The voice answered, 'Your brother will help you.'

'Oh my God,' Musa said, 'Make my heart strong. Make this easy for me.'

The voice said, 'I will make you both strong. Now go to the Pharaoh, together

with your brother, and speak to him about what he is doing. But speak to him gently. Maybe he will take a warning or maybe he will fear Allah.'

A message for the Pharaoh of Egypt

So Musa travelled to Egypt. There he met with his brother, Haroon.

Musa and Haroon prayed to Allah, 'Oh God! We are afraid that the Pharaoh will do bad things to us.'

Allah said to them, 'Don't be afraid, because I am with you. I hear and see everything. So both of you go, and bring to the Pharaoh my message.' And then Allah gave them the message.

So Musa and Haroon went to talk to the Pharaoh and his chief ministers. Musa said, 'We are messengers sent by the God of the Worlds. I have come with a clear sign. Send the Children of Israel with us, and let us all leave Egypt. Peace to everyone who follows His guidance. We have been shown that in the next life after death, those who did not believe and turned away from the truth will be punished. I can only say the truth about Allah.'

The Pharaoh was very surprised to see Musa and even more surprised to hear what he had to say.

The Pharaoh was angry. 'Who do you think you are? Didn't we keep you alive when you were a baby? Didn't you live with us in the palace for many years? And then you did that terrible thing when you killed the Egyptian.'

Musa made no excuses. 'Yes, I did it. And I was wrong. Then I ran away because I was afraid of you. But Allah gave me wisdom and made me one of his messengers. Anyway, look what you have done—you have made slaves of the Children of Israel.'

Teaching the Pharaoh

The Pharaoh had not heard anyone speak to him like this before. He was angry, but he had a question, too. These men were talking to him about Allah when he thought he himself was the god of Egypt. He asked Musa and Haroon, 'Who is this God you two have—the God of the Worlds?'

Then Musa and Haroon started to explain. 'Our God is the God of the heavens and the earth and all that is between them; the One who made everything in the world. He has a plan for everything and everyone.'

The Pharaoh said, 'If there is only one God like you say, then what about all the people in the past who worshipped many gods?'

Musa answered, 'Only Allah knows. Allah knows everything that has happened in the past and never makes a mistake, never forgets.'

Musa said, 'Allah knows who follows His guidance and who will have the best end in the life after death. It is certain that the people who do wrong will not have a good end.'

The Pharaoh turned to the people around him and asked, 'Did you hear what they said?'

'He is your God, too. And the God of your ancestors, right from the beginning,' said Musa.

The Pharaoh was scornful. 'This messenger who has been sent to you is a crazy man.'

Musa said, 'He is God of the East and God of the West, and everything in between. If only you had sense!'

The Pharaoh said, 'If you choose to worship any god other than me, I will certainly throw you in prison!'

Musa asked, 'Even if I showed you something that will make it very clear?'

The Pharaoh said, 'Show it then, if you are telling the truth.'

So Musa threw down his walking stick. And look—it was a snake. Everyone could see it. He raised his hand up from near his heart, and look—it was bright and shining for everyone to see.

The Pharaoh said, 'Such magic! Have you come to turn us away from the ways we found our fathers following so that you and your brother might become popular here? We won't believe in you!'

Musa said to the Pharaoh, 'How can you say this after you've seen the signs from Allah? Is this magic? Magicians never win.'

The king was now surprised and a bit worried. He had a meeting with his chief ministers. 'This is certainly a very clever magician. He has a plan to get you out of Egypt with his magic. So then what do you suggest?'

The ministers said, 'Let him and his brother wait. Send men to all the cities of Egypt to find all the best magicians and bring them back here.'

Contest with the magicians

The best magicians in the land were brought together on a festival day, to have a contest with Musa and Haroon. When huge crowds of people had gathered, the people were asked: ‘Are you all ready? Are you ready to believe in the magicians if they win?’

When the magicians came, they asked the Pharaoh, ‘Will we have a reward if we win?’

The Pharaoh said, ‘Yes, you will be given a big reward, and more—you will become almost as important as I in this country.’

Musa said to them, ‘Your turn is first. Throw whatever it is that you will throw.’

So the magicians threw their ropes and their sticks, and showed all the people the magic they could do. Their ropes wriggled and squirmed like snakes. They said, ‘Look! With the power of the Pharaoh, we will be the winners!’

Musa saw their magic and he was afraid. Then Allah spoke to him and made his heart strong. ‘Do not be afraid. You are the one who will really win. Now throw down the walking stick which is in your right hand. It will swallow what they have done, because what they have done is only a magician’s trick. And a magician will never really win, no matter what he tries to do.’

Then Musa threw down his walking stick, and look—the snake immediately ate up all the trick snakes.

Everyone was amazed. The magicians knew Musa was not playing tricks. What Musa had done was real. It was the God of Musa and Haroon that had done it. The magicians fell down on the ground, bowing down to Allah, saying, ‘We believe in the God of the Universe, the God of Musa and Haroon.’

The Pharaoh was very angry. ‘Are you going to believe in this other God before I give you permission? This must be a trick of yours, to drive the people out of the city. But soon you will know.’ And then the Pharaoh threatened them. ‘I will cut off your hands and your feet on opposite sides, and I will hang you all to die on a cross.’

But the magicians knew the truth now. There was only one God and the Pharaoh was just a wicked man. They said, ‘It doesn’t matter. We will just return to Allah.’

The Pharaoh had thought the magicians would fall down before him and cry for forgiveness. But here they were talking like this. And they said, ‘You are angry with us because we believed in Allah’s signs when they came to us. We now believe in Allah who made us. We hope He will forgive what we have done wrong and the magic you made us do, and pray that he will take us as believers.’

The Pharaoh doesn't listen

After this, Musa went on trying to make the Pharaoh understand. But the Pharaoh did not want to listen. He turned away from the message which Musa had brought from Allah. He and his chief ministers all said, 'All this is just some kind of magic. We've never heard about anything like this before.'

The Pharaoh had a meeting with his ministers. He said to them, 'I am your god. You have no other god but me.'

And he said to Haman, one of his chief ministers, 'Start building a high tower. Make it of clay bricks. Build it so high that I can go up to see the God of Musa. As far as I know, Musa is a liar.'

Haman built a tower, a very high tower, but he could never build it high enough. Haman and his workers grew tired.

The Pharaoh's ministers were upset. They knew that Musa had asked for all the Children of Israel —their slaves—to leave Egypt. They said to the Pharaoh, 'Are you going to let Musa and his people make trouble in this country? Are you going to let them leave you and your gods?'

Pharaoh made a decision. 'Let me kill Musa and then let him call to his Lord. I am afraid that he will change the religion in Egypt or upset our kingdom.'

The Pharaoh of Egypt made life harder and harder for the Children of Israel. And he made plans to kill Musa.

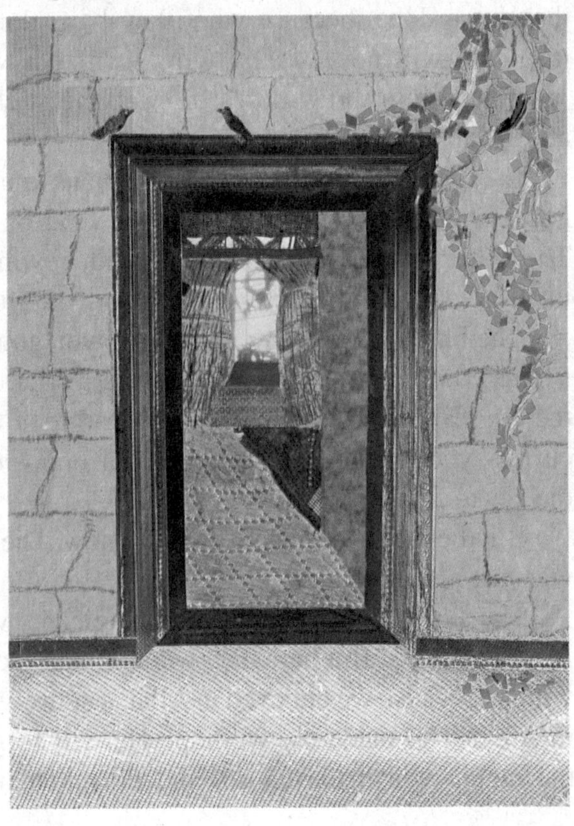

Pharaoh's wife believes

Many years before when baby Musa had been pulled from the Nile River in his floating box, it was the wife of Pharaoh who had wanted to keep him, and she had saved his life. She had cared for him as he grew up and had loved him as her own son.

Now that Musa had returned to Egypt and was telling the Pharaoh about the Lord of the Universe, she understood. She did not believe her powerful husband, who kept telling people to worship him. She believed that Musa was a messenger of God, and that Allah was the only God. So even though Pharaoh had power over his wife and what she did, he had no power over her heart and mind.

She prayed, 'My Lord, build me a house with You in the Garden. Save me from Pharaoh and what he does and save me, too, from the people who do bad things.'

Allah made an example of Pharaoh's wife for those who believe.

An Egyptian believer

There was another man among the people of the Pharaoh who also secretly believed in Allah. At last he talked to the Egyptians. He said, 'Are you going to kill a man because he says he believes in Allah and shows you clear signs from Allah? If he is lying, that's his problem. But if he is telling the truth, then the terrible things he talks about will fall on you. Really, Allah doesn't help people who are liars. Oh' my people! These days you are strong in this land, but who will help us if Allah sends us bad times?'

The Pharaoh said, 'I understand everything, and the way I see things is just the way I tell you. I tell you what to believe.'

Then the believer said, 'Oh my people! I am afraid that terrible things will happen to you. Remember what happened to the people of Nuh, to the people of Ad and to the people of Thamood. I am afraid there will be a time when you will all cry and run, and no one will be able to help you. Many years ago, Yusuf came here and told our people about Allah, and it was clear what we should believe. After he died, the people said, Allah won't send another messenger.'

The Pharaoh and his people didn't want to listen to this Egyptian. But the man who believed in Allah kept on talking, 'Oh my people! Listen to me. I will lead you to the right path. What's happening these days is nothing. What is important is the life hereafter. Whoever does wrong things will have great trouble, but the men and women who believe and do good things will live in a wonderful garden filled with wonderful things. It is certain that we all return to Allah when we die. If you don't listen to me now, you will soon remember what I've said.'

The Pharaoh and his people had no ears for what this man had to say. They made all sorts of plans to hurt him, but Allah kept him safe.

Teaching the Children of Israel

During this time, Musa and Haroon spent a great deal of time with the Children of Israel. They talked to them about Allah. For all their troubles, they said, 'Ask Allah for help and be patient. Remember, the whole earth belongs to Allah, and He gives it to His followers if He pleases.'

But the Israelites were miserable. They felt terrible. Since Musa had started talking to the Pharaoh, everything had become worse. They were very tired of the way they had to live. They complained to Musa, 'We've had nothing but trouble since you came to us.'

But Musa told them to be patient and to trust Allah. 'Maybe Allah will destroy your enemy and make you leaders on this earth. He is going to see whatever you do now.'

Terrible times in Egypt

Allah began to show His great power to the Pharaoh of Egypt and his ministers. One disaster after another came to the people of Egypt. There were years without rain and the crops were poor. The people of Egypt said it was because of the bad things Musa had done. Whenever something good happened, they said, 'This is because of us.' But when something bad happened, they blamed Musa. 'Whatever magic you work on us, we will never believe in you.'

More disasters came to Egypt. Floods covered the land. Many people and animals died. Swarms of locusts ate all the plants. Lice bothered everyone. Frogs were everywhere. Water turned into blood.

Every time a disaster came, the Egyptians asked Musa to pray to Allah to take it away from them, and that if He did, they would believe in Musa and let the Israelites leave Egypt with him. But every time Allah took away the disaster, they broke their promises. And the Pharaoh and his chief ministers continued to be proud and stubborn and mean to the Israelites, and did not listen to the warnings that Allah sent to them.

Learning to trust Allah

Only some of the Children of Israel were believing in what Musa had to say. Others were afraid of the Pharaoh of Egypt and his chief ministers. The Pharaoh would get very angry with the Israelites and, because they were afraid, they obeyed him. But Musa went on preaching to his people. 'Oh my people. If you really believe in Allah, put your trust in Him.'

The people answered Musa, 'We do trust in Allah.' And they prayed, 'Do not put us to a test with these bad people and save us from people who do not believe.'

Allah gave Musa and Haroon instructions that the people should arrange some houses where they would have regular prayers. Musa was told to give the believers the good news that Allah was with them and that He would help them.

Then Musa prayed to Allah: 'Oh our God! You have given the Pharaoh of Egypt and the chief ministers power and riches in this world. With it they are leading the people away from Your path. Oh God, wipe out their riches and make their hearts hard and do not let them believe. Let them see the terrible punishment that is waiting for them.'

Allah answered, 'Your prayer is accepted, Oh Musa and Haroon. Keep on with your work, both of you, and do not follow the path of those who do not know.'

Time to leave Egypt

Then one day Allah's command came to Musa. 'It is time to go. Travel with my followers, the Children of Israel, by night, and open up a path for them through the sea. Do not worry that you will be overtaken. And do not be afraid.'

Musa got his people ready to leave Egypt. There were so many of them. They had to leave behind their homes, and most of their things. They took what they would need for travelling, just what they could carry. Then, as quietly as possible, the Children of Israel crept out of the city in the darkness of the night.

The next morning, the Egyptians saw that the Israelites had left the city during the night. The Pharaoh of Egypt was very angry. He and his army chased after them, planning to kill them or to take them back as their slaves. They caught up with the Israelites the next morning, at sunrise, at the shore of the sea.

When the people following Musa saw the army, they were very afraid. In front of them was the sea; behind them was an army ready to capture them. They cried, 'We will surely be captured!'

Musa said to them, 'No, we will not be captured. Never. Allah is with us, and He will guide us.'

Then Allah gave Musa instructions. 'Strike the water with your walking stick.' Musa raised his stick to the water, and immediately the water of the sea divided into two parts, with a dry path between the two walls of water on either side. Musa led the people through the sea, and they started to walk safely to the other shore.

The Pharaoh of Egypt and his army followed the Israelites down the dry path between the walls of water. Meanwhile, Musa and his people had crossed over to the other side. When the army was in the middle of the sea, the walls of water suddenly broke and came crashing down on top of it. All the men and animals were caught in the rushing water. They cried for help. Musa and Haroon and all their followers were safe on the other side and could hear them screaming.

The Pharaoh of Egypt finally believed what Musa had been telling him. He finally believed that Allah was more powerful and greater than he. The Pharaoh was afraid of dying, and he wanted to be saved. He cried, 'I believe that there is no God other than the God of the Children of Israel, and I am one of the believers.' But it was too late. The Pharaoh of Egypt and all his army drowned in the sea.

Some of the Israelites who remembered the great power of Pharaoh wondered if he had really died. But when his body was washed up on the shore they were sure that he was dead. How many gardens, springs of water, croplands and wonderful things Pharaoh and his armies had left behind! Just like that, it was all given to other people, and no one was sad and cried for them. Allah said that the dead body of Pharaoh was a sign for those who would follow him.

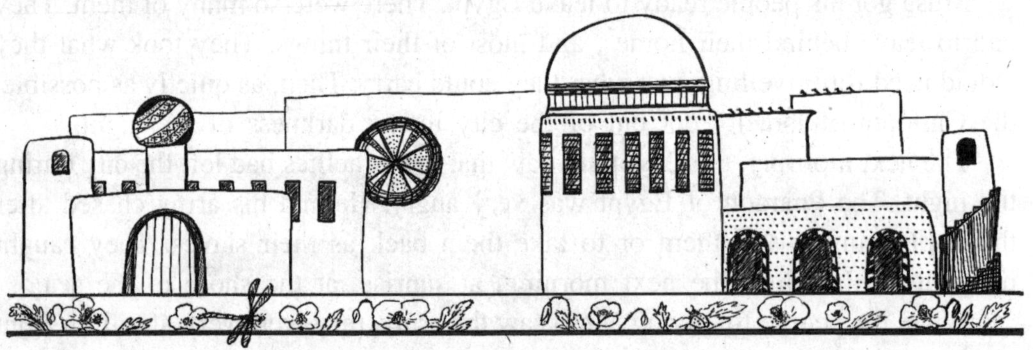

Free at last

The Children of Israel were safe. They had left Egypt, crossed the sea, and had seen the Pharaoh of Egypt and his army destroyed. Now they were free.

Musa and Haroon were their two leaders, and they followed them into the hot dry desert. They had no food with them, but Allah helped them. Allah gave them manna, which they could pick up in the desert every morning. He gave them salwa, which were small birds that they could catch and eat. And Allah made the clouds in the sky to give them shade from the burning sun.

When they were thirsty and the people asked for water, Allah told Musa 'Hit the rock with your walking stick', and the water came gushing out of the rocks in twelve different places. There were twelve different family groups of people, and then each group had their own place to get water.

Allah had a plan for the Children of Israel. When they would be ready to follow His guidance completely, they would return to the land which Allah had given to Prophet Ibraheem. That was the land where Ishaq and Yaqoob had lived, and from where Yaqoob's family had travelled to live with Yusuf in Egypt.

But the Children of Israel were a confused people. They had lived in Egypt for a long time among people who did not believe in Allah and who had worshipped idols. As they travelled in the desert they saw other people worshipping idols, too, and they wanted to do the same thing. They forgot how Allah had saved them from their life of slavery with the Egyptians. They said to Musa, 'Oh Musa, set up an idol for us to worship, like other people have.'

Musa was very angry. 'You are a people with no sense. The way these people live here is not good. In the end, they will be destroyed. Just remember how Allah rescued you from the Egyptians, who treated you so badly, who killed your baby boys and kept alive the baby girls. Allah has chosen to help you, above all other people. And you ask me to find another god for you to worship?'

Musa goes up on the mountain

The people kept travelling through the desert. Musa led them toward the mountain where Allah had spoken to him a long, long time ago. When they came near to the mountain, Allah told Musa to prepare to go up on the mountain, away from the people. He would be gone for forty nights. So Musa told Haroon to stay with the people. 'Be their leader while I am gone. Make sure you don't listen to the people who are doing bad things.' They all made their camp at the bottom of the mountain, and Musa climbed the mountain.

Allah spoke to Musa up on the mountain. Musa wanted very much to see Allah with his own eyes, and said, 'Oh my God! Show Yourself to me so that I may look at You.' Allah answered him, 'You cannot see Me, but look at the mountain. If it stays in its place, then you will be able to look at Me.'

When Allah showed Himself, it was so powerful that the rocks of the mountain turned to powder, and Musa could not stand on his feet. He fell down in a daze and couldn't see, couldn't hear, couldn't keep his balance. Allah's presence was too powerful for a man to be near to Him.

When Musa could finally speak, he said to Allah, ' Glory to You! I am sorry for what I said, and I am the first among those who believe.'

'Oh Musa!' Allah said, ' I have chosen you above all other people, for the words I have spoken to you and for the work that you must do. Now be thankful and take my message.'

Allah then gave Musa laws to tell the people how they should live. They were written on stone tablets. The laws were about everything—what they should and should not do, and explained everything for how to live as a believer. He said to Musa, 'Take these laws. Tell your people to follow the laws and be strong in this good way of life.'

The golden calf

Musa had a very big job to do. He had to teach Allah's law to his people. He had been up on the mountain for forty days and nights. When it was time for him to go back down to his people with the law, Allah warned him that while he had been gone, the people had gone through a test, and had made mistakes. A man named Samiri had told them to do bad things.

When Musa came down into the camp at the bottom of the mountain, he saw a golden statue of a calf standing there. His people were all around the golden calf, worshipping it. They had made an idol.

Musa was angry. He was furious. And he was sad. The people had told Musa before he went up on the mountain that they were believers and would be good while he was gone. What had they done? Musa cried, 'Oh my people! Didn't Allah promise you a good life? Was it taking too long? Or did you want Allah to be angry with you, and so you broke your promise to me?'

The people answered, 'We didn't break our promise to you because we wanted to do bad things. But we were carrying so much heavy gold, we melted it all down in a fire. That is what Samiri told us to do. And then Samiri made this statue of a calf. And it even seemed to make the sound of a calf, saying moo-ooo.'

The people had thought Samiri's magic was wonderful. They liked the golden calf, and he had told them that the calf was their god. Musa had made Haroon their leader while he was gone, and Haroon had tried to tell them such idol worship was wrong. Haroon had said, 'Oh people! Listen to me! You are being tested. You have only one God. Worship Allah.'

But the people had not listened to Haroon. They had said, 'We won't stop worshipping this golden calf until Musa comes back to us.'

Misled by Samiri

So now Musa had come back, with a great message from Allah for them, and he found the people worshipping an idol. 'What a terrible thing you have done while I was away! Have you forgotten Allah?'

Musa put down the stone tablets on which the Law of Allah was written. He was so angry that he took hold of his brother Haroon by the hair and pulled him. 'Oh Haroon! Why did you let them do this? Why didn't you obey what I had said?'

Haroon said, 'Oh son of my mother! Don't pull my beard or the hair on my head! I was really afraid that you would say I had made this trouble among the Children of Israel and that I had not listened to you. They almost killed me! Don't think I am among those who did this terrible thing.'

Then Musa prayed, 'Oh my God! Forgive me and my brother!'

Musa turned to the Israelites and said, 'My people, you have done something terrible against yourselves with this calf. So those of you who did not worship this calf, kill those who did worship it. And remember Allah.'

Then Musa called the man named Samiri to him, 'What do you have to say, Samiri?'

Samiri said, 'I saw what the people couldn't see. So I took a handful of dust from the footprint of God's messenger and threw it into the melted gold for the calf. That's the idea that I had.'

Musa said, 'Get away from here! From now on in this life you will live alone and no one will come near you. It will be worse for you in the next life. And now look at that idol you worship. It will be melted in a fire and thrown in the sea.'

Then, when he was not so angry any more, Musa picked up the stone tablets with the Law of Allah. He said to the people, 'Allah is your God. There is no other god, and His knowledge is everything.' Allah's anger would be on those who worshipped the calf as their god. But for those who saw that they had done wrong and really believed in Allah, Allah would forgive them. The people said, 'Unless Allah forgives us, we will really be lost.'

Learning the law

Then Musa took the stone tablets. Musa chose seventy leaders from among the Children of Israel, and took them up on the mountain to ask for forgiveness and to learn about the Law which Allah had given them.

Up there on the mountain they said to Musa, 'We won't believe what you say until we see Allah with our own eyes!' When they said that, the mountain started to shake, like an earthquake.

Musa prayed, 'Oh my God! If You had wanted to do it, You could have destroyed them and me, too. Will you destroy us because of the things the foolish ones among us do? This is another test, and with it You make clear who will not follow You and whom You lead on the right path. You are our Protector, so forgive us, because we believe in You.'

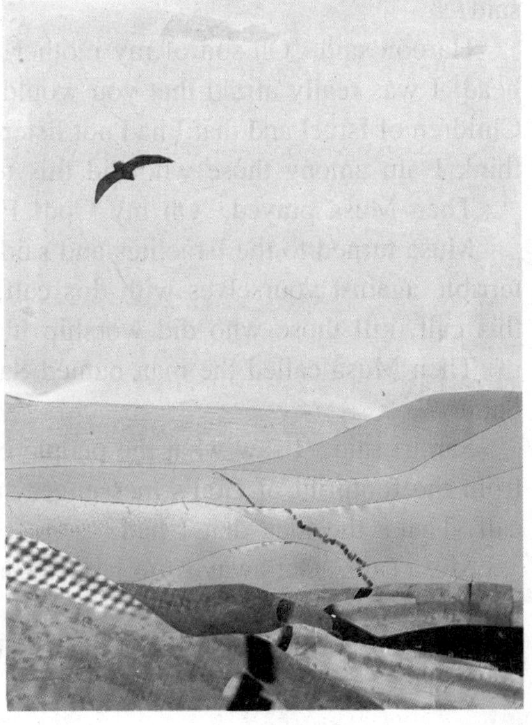

Allah answered Musa, 'My Mercy is for everything. It is for those who do what is right, who help others, who believe in the signs in this world, who follow the messengers. The messages they bring tell the people what is right and what is wrong. The believers will always be helped. They will be made strong and will follow the Light which is sent down with the messenger.'

After many days, they all went down from the mountain.

The right path

The Children of Israel had a hard time following the right path. Allah was merciful to them, and kept showing

them the good way to live. From the beginning, Allah had given them the right religion. He had brought them out of slavery in Egypt and away from the bad Pharaoh of Egypt and the people who worshipped idols in Egypt. He kept them alive in the desert, with clouds for shade from the sun, with water to drink for all twelve of their huge families, and with food to eat.

Musa was disturbed by the way the people were not strong believers in their hearts. He had tried to lead them just as Allah had told him.

Qarun's end

There was a man among the people named Qarun. He had been rich in Egypt and was the leader of a big group of people. But Qarun had to leave all his riches behind when the Children of Israel left Egypt. He had brought the keys to all his treasure chests along. The keys were big and heavy, and he walked around showing off his keys.

Some of the people said to Qarun, 'Don't be so proud. Allah doesn't love people who are so happy with money and things. You should be happy with the promise of Allah's riches in the life after death. And don't forget that Allah has been good to you and you should also do good things.'

Qarun said, 'All these riches are mine because of everything that I know.' And he went around showing off his glitter.

Many persons who saw him were jealous. Some of them said, 'I wish I had what Qarun has.'

But those people who really knew said to him, 'Too bad for you. Allah's reward in life after death is for those who believe in Him and do good.'

Qarun did not listen to them and did not change his ways. He went from bad to worse. Then one day, Allah made something terrible happen to him. The earth started to move and Qarun and everything he owned were pulled into the ground. No one could help him. The ground fell in on top of him and he was buried.

The people, who the day before had been jealous of Qarun, then changed the way they talked. They said, 'Ah yes! It is Allah who gives us things and takes them away. If Allah wasn't so good to us, He could have made the earth swallow us up, too! Oh my! Those who turn away from Allah will never have a good end.'

Complaining people

One day, the people called Musa and said, 'Look here, Musa—we are sick of eating just one kind of food. So call on your God and ask Him to give us some other plants out of the ground, like the herbs and cucumbers and corn and lentils and onions.'

Musa was disgusted. He said, 'Do you want to give up something so great for something that means nothing? Go back to Egypt, then, and you can have all that you're asking for.'

The people were ashamed of themselves.

When they came near to a city they wanted to settle down to enjoy the comfortable life of a town, and they were told by Allah, 'Go into the town to eat whatever you like. When you go through the gates of the city, go humbly and say, 'We will change our ways'.

Then the people were angry with this command from Allah and didn't want to go into the town. They changed the words they were supposed to say, and then many bad things happened to them.

But the Children of Israel kept on doing things that were not right, and would not obey Allah. Their hearts were not open to Allah's messages for them. Their hearts became hard, as hard as rocks. So the Children of Israel kept wandering about in the desert for many years without a home.

Slaughter a cow!

Allah told Musa to tell his people to slaughter a cow. Before, the people had worshipped an idol that looked like a cow, and many people in Egypt and around them here in the desert worshipped cows in their religion. So when Musa went to the people and said, 'Allah tells you to slaughter a young cow', they said, 'Are you joking?' Why would Allah ask us to do such a thing?

But Musa said, 'I ask Allah to save me from being foolish.'

The people said, 'Ask your God to show us clearly which young cow it should be.'

Musa answered, 'He says the cow should be not too old or too young, but in between. Now do what you are told.'

The people said, 'Ask your God to show us clearly what colour she should be.'

Musa answered, 'He says the cow should be a beautiful light brown colour, so that whoever looks at the cow will admire her.'

The people said, 'Ask your God to show us clearly which cow it is. To us, all young cows are the same. We want God's help in choosing.'

Musa answered, 'He says she should not be a cow that has worked in the fields. She should be strong and without any poor markings.'

The people then said, 'If Allah wills, we will be guided.'

And then the people unwillingly took such a perfect young cow and slaughtered it. They didn't want to do it.

The promised land

After a long time in the desert, Musa thought that finally his people might be ready to go into the land that Allah had promised the Prophet Ibraheem. Musa said to the people, 'Oh my people, remember how Allah has chosen you to be

his special people. He put prophets among you and gave you what He gave no one else in the world. Now it is time to go into the holy land which Allah has promised you.' A group of twelve men was sent to the land which Allah had promised to the Children of Israel, to see what was there and who lived there. They came back with stories about a beautiful land and very strong people. They brought delicious fruits to eat—pomegranates and figs and grapes.

The Children of Israel were afraid when they heard about the people who lived there. They said, 'Oh Musa! There are people that live in that land who are very, very strong. We'll never go there until they have left. If ever they go out, then we will go in.'

Musa said to them, 'You must trust Allah completely. Go into the land you have been promised. But do not turn back. If you do, you will lose.'

Two of the men who had gone as spies were strong believers and they spoke. They had a plan. They said to the people, 'Just go into the city gate. Once you are in, you will win. But you must trust Allah if you are really believers.'

The people answered, 'Oh Musa! If those people are there, we will never be able to enter. No—not till the end of time. So you go, you and your God, and you two can fight while we will sit here and watch.'

Musa had had enough. He was finished with the people. He said, 'My God, I have no control over anyone else except myself and my brother. So separate us from these bad people.'

Allah answered Musa. 'Because of this, the land will be forbidden to the Children of Israel for forty years, and they will have to wander around in the desert all that time. Do not worry about these people who do so many wrong things.'

The story of Musa

So this is the story of Musa, Allah's special messenger to the Children of Israel.

From the time he was saved as a baby on the River Nile, growing up in the palace of the Pharaoh of Egypt and running for his life into the Madyan Desert, Allah was preparing Musa to be a leader of his people.

On Mount Toor, Allah called Musa to take His message to the Pharaoh of Egypt, so he went back to Egypt where he had grown up. There he started to teach his own people about Allah. His people were slaves to the Egyptians and many had forgotten about Allah. Together with his brother Haroon, with Allah's guidance, Musa taught the Children of Israel to believe in Allah and how to worship

Him with regular prayers. Musa and Haroon worked very hard, trying to teach the Pharaoh of Egypt and his people about Allah, too, but only a few believed. Musa brought nine clear signs to the Pharaoh of Egypt, to show who was the God of the Heavens and the Earth: his walking stick, his shining hand, the years when there was no water in Egypt, the poor crops, the widespread deaths among people and their animals, the locusts, the lice, the frogs and the water turning into blood. But the Pharaoh said it was all just magic. Musa knew the Pharaoh would be destroyed, and that is what happened. The Pharaoh met with his end, together with his whole army, in the depths of sea. And the Children of Israel were free at last.

Musa led the Children of Israel out of Egypt into the desert, back to the mountain where Allah had first spoken to him. And that is where Allah gave them the Law for their lives and taught them how to follow the right path. But the Children of Israel had to learn many lessons. And so it was forty years before the Children of Israel entered the land they were promised. By that time both Musa and Haroon had died.

This story about Prophet Musa is found in the Noble Qur'an in many different Surahs:

2:49-71	10:75-92	23:45-9	43:46-56
4:164	17:101-4	28:3-46,76-82	44:17-32
5:22-9	18:60-82	37:112-22	66:11
7:103-56	20:9-104	40:23-45	79:15-26

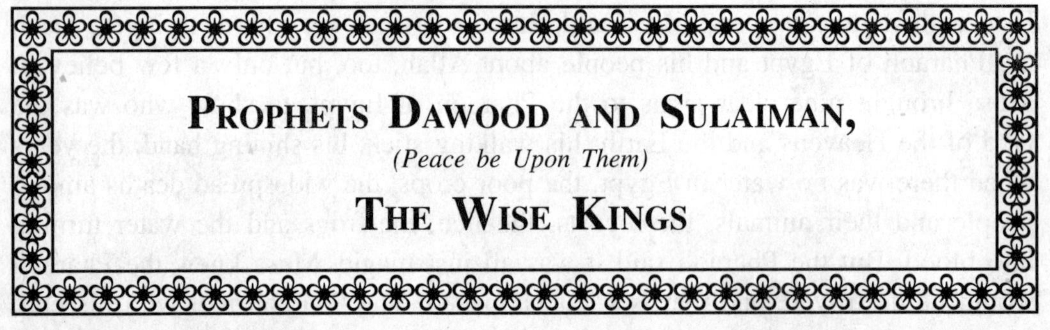

PROPHETS DAWOOD AND SULAIMAN,
(Peace be Upon Them)
THE WISE KINGS

Dawood praises Allah

A long time ago, the Children of Israel had a wise king named Dawood. He would pray to Allah at dawn, just when the sun would come up. He would also pray in the fading light of the evening, when the birds would fly and gather together to sing their songs.

Allah had given Dawood the gift of music and told all of nature to join him in his worship. 'Oh you mountains! Echo the praises of God with him! And you birds, sing too!' At these times when the hills around him were beautiful and alive with the light of sunrise and sunset, the hills and the birds all joined together with King Dawood to praise Allah.

Dawood the shepherd

As a boy, Dawood had been a shepherd. He had spent his days out under the skies with his sheep. He was strong. And he always thought of Allah. He loved to sing praises to Allah when he was out in the hills.

Dawood the warrior

When Dawood was a young man, Talut was the king of the Israelites. Another name for him was King Jalut. There was an army set to fight the Israelites. They were led by a man named Jalut, also known as Talut. Jalut was a huge and fearful leader of the enemy.

King Talut gathered his forces together and prepared to fight the army that was coming. Dawood also went along to fight Talut and his men.

To make sure that everyone in King Talut's forces would be faithful, the men were given a test. They were given a certain order at the river. King Talut told them, 'Allah will test you at the river. If you drink the water, you will not go to fight. Only those who don't drink will go. Just sipping some water out of your hand will be excused.' When they crossed the river, all but a few of the men drank the water. So it was clear who would be faithful to Allah.

The few who were faithful crossed the river. Dawood was with them. But they were afraid of the strong army. They said, 'Today we can not meet with Talut and his army.'

But some were sure that they should go on. They said, 'How often, with Allah's power, has a small army overtaken a big one? God is with those who are faithful.'

When they met Talut and his army, they prayed, 'Our God! Make us strong and our steps sure. Help us against those who do not believe in Allah.'

It was an amazing battle. With Allah's will, they won. And it was Dawood who killed Talut.

Dawood the king

After the battle with Talut, everyone knew about Dawood. He was later chosen to be the king for the Children of Israel.

Allah gave Dawood power and wisdom and taught him whatever he wanted to know. Whatever he did and whatever he learned, King Dawood praised Allah. These praises were all put together in the Book of Dawood called Zabur.

Allah taught Dawood how to make coats of armour. He showed Dawood how to make the iron soft, so that it could be moulded. Then He made iron rings to fit into each other like a chain, which were made into coats for the men when they had to fight in a battle. Allah said to Dawood, 'Make sure that you balance the rings of chain armour well. And make sure that you and your people act well. Your fighting is only to protect what is right. Don't be violent. You can all be sure that I clearly see everything that you do.'

King Dawood had a son. His name was Sulaiman. Sulaiman would grow up to take the throne when his father died, and he learned all about the kingdom in his young years.

King Dawood was a wise king. Whenever people in the kingdom had a problem that they couldn't settle, they would come to the King and he would make the decisions for them.

One day, two men came to King Dawood with their problem. The one man pointed to the other and said, 'My crops have been destroyed by his sheep. They came on to my fields during the night.'

King Dawood thought carefully about their problem and said to the owner of the sheep, 'You should pay this man who lost his crops by giving him the sheep.'

Sulaiman, still a young boy at the time, was listening. He had a better suggestion. Sulaiman said, 'The owner of the field should not get the sheep to keep as his own. He should only take them for a while until the damage is repaid. The owner of the field could use the milk, the wool, and maybe keep some lambs, but then the sheep should be returned to the shepherd. Otherwise the shepherd will have nothing.'

Young Sulaiman's suggestion decided the matter. And he showed how wise he already was.

King Dawood's lesson

King Dawood prayed at regular times in a room by himself.

One day, he thought he saw two men climbing over the wall into his room. He was frightened by them. But the men said to him, 'Don't be afraid. We have come here to ask you to help us. We have a quarrel and we want you to decide something for us. Treat us fairly and show us what is right.'

The man who felt he was being mistreated pointed to the other and said, 'This man is my brother. We are shepherds. He has ninety-nine ewes and I have only one. And he says I have to give her to him. He speaks to me badly. What shall I do?'

King Dawood answered, 'He is clearly doing something wrong, by asking for your one ewe to be added to his large flock.'

Then he went on saying, 'There are many people who work together who are not fair to each other. This never happens among the people who really believe and do good things. But how many people are like this?'

Then suddenly King Dawood realized this was a dream. There were no two men with him in his room. And he understood that this had been a lesson and a test for him. He felt bad, because he saw how proud he always was of himself and his own good deeds. He fell down to the ground, bowing low. He was sorry for his self-pride and asked Allah to forgive him.

Allah did forgive him and King Dawood was promised that after he died, he would be in a beautiful place near to Allah.

And Allah said to him, 'Oh Dawood, you are really in charge of others on earth. So be a judge of men who is honest and fair. Don't be tempted by things that would lead you away from the path of Allah.'

Father to son

The Kingdom of Dawood became strong, with Allah's help. Allah gave King Dawood wisdom in what he said and in the decisions he made. He taught his son Sulaiman everything he knew. They both knew that their knowledge, wisdom and power came from Allah. They said, 'Praise be to Allah, who has chosen us above many of His followers!'

When King Dawood died, Sulaiman was ready to take over the throne.

Sulaiman the lover of Nature

King Sulaiman understood things about all creatures—about where they lived, how they found their food and how they talked to each other. He knew about birds and animals and plants and could understand their languages.

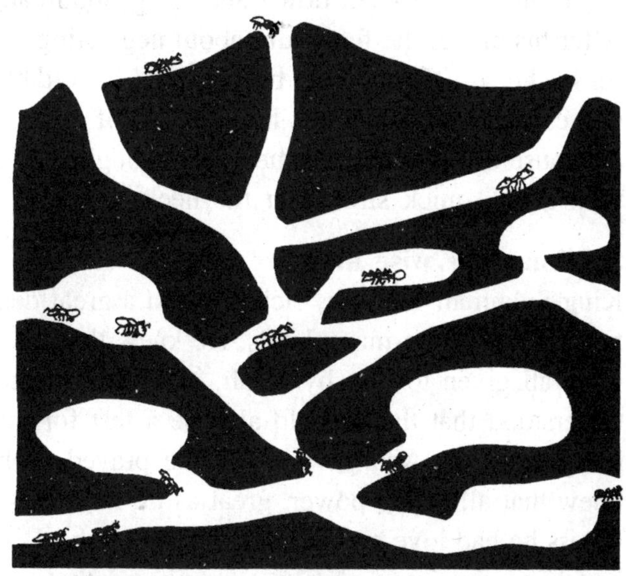

King Sulaiman was thankful to God for being able to understand so much. In his prayers to God he said, 'Make me thankful for all the gifts which You have given to me and my parents. Help me to live in a good way.' Because he was so wise and could communicate with all living things, many people thought King Sulaiman was doing magic. But they were wrong. His power came from Allah.

King Sulaiman said to his people, 'We have been given a little understanding of all things. This is a gift from God for us, for which we should all be thankful.'

King Sulaiman liked to go through the fields and forests, where he could watch the animals and study the plants.

Once when King Sulaiman came to a colony of ants, busy at their work, one of the ants said to the others, 'All you ants—go into your homes quickly, so that King Sulaiman and his many men don't step on you with their feet.' So the ants scurried into their homes.

King Sulaiman heard the ant say this. He smiled and said to Allah, 'Oh my God! Teach me to walk carefully and to do the right work everywhere I go.'

A test

King Sulaiman was fond of horses. One evening, just before sunset, several excellent war charriot horses were brought to him. They were coarsers—graceful horses that would stand on three legs, with their fourth hoof just resting lightly on the ground. They could run like the wind. As he admired his horses, he said, 'I really love what is the very best, a love that sees Allah's glory in everything.'

Then the sun went down and King Sulaiman was late in saying his prayers. After his prayer, he felt badly about neglecting his prayer. He returned and called for his horses. 'Bring them back to me,' he told his helpers. His love for his horses had caused him to neglect his worship of Allah, and so he decided to get rid of the cause of his neglect. When they brought the beautiful animals, he killed them with a few quick strokes at the neck.

Sulaiman the wise king

King Sulaiman was very rich. He had a great deal of power in his kingdom, and he was famous in many lands. He knew that his wealth, his power and his glory were all given to him by Allah, just like his knowledge about all creatures. He understood that these could also be a test for him. He might be tempted to use his gifts in the wrong way. And he prayed, 'Oh my God, forgive me.' But he knew that all of his power, great as he was, was like a dead body on his throne, unless he had love and guidance from Allah. His highest reward was with Allah, and King Sulaiman always remembered that.

King Sulaiman asked Allah, 'Give me special powers in my kingdom. I will not use them in a wrong way. It may be that the king who follows me will not be able to use such power in the right ways, but I ask this because You are the Giver of Gifts without end.'

And so King Sulaiman was given power over many beings, like jinns and people and birds, and they were all given their places and kept in order. They worked for King Sulaiman as he ordered them, building arches and carving statues. A fountain of molten brass flowed for King Sulaiman and they pounded the brass into huge dishes and made big cooking pots, so heavy that they had to be fixed in their places. When people were given their many different kinds of jobs, they went to work. But the jinns had to work under King Sulaiman's constantly watchful eye. Some of the jinns were good, others were bad. Most of the bad ones worked for King Sulaiman as builders and divers. And Allah guarded over them all.

Most of the people worked together well, and were happy in their work. But most of the jinns did not like to work. Allah said, 'Work, members of the House of Dawood, with thankfulness. Few of my other servants are thankful.'

King Sulaiman was also given power over the wind. He could make it blow wherever and however he ordered it to blow. The wind's speed in the early morning and in the evening could cover the same distance as what could be travelled in a month. When the wind was terrible and strong, King Sulaiman would make it blow gently.

The hoopoe brings news

One day King Sulaiman called the birds together, and he did not see the hoopoe who worked as his scout. The hoopoe was a beautiful bird of many colours, with a yellow crown of feathers on his head.

King Sulaiman said, 'Why don't I see the hoopoe? Is he among the birds that are out flying? He will certainly be in trouble with me if he doesn't have a good reason for being away right now.'

The hoopoe came back soon. He flew up to King Sulaiman and said to him, 'I have seen a land far away. And I have come with news from a place called Saba. I found a woman there who is the queen of a wonderful land. She has everything she needs, and she has a beautiful throne.'

'She and her people worship the sun. They think what they're doing is right. Satan has kept them away from the right path and so they get no help. They do not worship God who shows us what is hidden in the heavens and the earth and knows everything about everyone.'

A letter for the Queen of Saba

King Sulaiman said to the hoopoe, 'Soon we'll know if you're telling us the truth.'

Then King Sulaiman wrote a message on a paper and gave it to the hoopoe. 'Go with this letter of mine, and take it to the people in Saba. Then wait there a while to hear their answer.' So the hoopoe took the letter to the Queen of Saba.

When the Queen of Saba received the letter, she said to her chief ministers, 'Look here. Here is an important letter from King Sulaiman. This is what it says:

'*Bismillah-ir-Rahman-ir-Raheem.*

Do not be proud.

Come to me with a true understanding of God.'

The Queen said, 'You chief ministers! What do you think about this? Give me some advice. I have never decided things without your help.'

They talked about how King Sulaiman might come with an army to take over the land of Saba. The chief ministers told the Queen, 'Our army is strong. It is ready to fight in war. But you give the orders. Decide what you will.'

Gifts for King Sulaiman

The Queen of Saba said, 'When kings enter a country, they destroy it and the best of its people act in terrible ways. I will send King Sulaiman some splendid gifts and wait to see what answer my ambassadors bring back.'

So the ambassadors went to King Sulaiman with the gifts from the Queen.

When they arrived, King Sulaiman said, 'Are you bringing me rich gifts? What

God has given me is much richer than what he has given you. Did you think I wanted gifts? No—it is *you* who are happy with your gifts. Go back to Saba and be sure that we will come there with a huge army. We'll take over the land and the people will feel very humble.'

Preparing for the Queen

When the ambassadors returned to the kingdom of Saba, the Queen and her people prepared to go to meet King Sulaiman. She had thought about the letter for a long while, and she had decided to go to see King Sulaiman. She understood that it was wrong to worship the sun and wanted to learn more about Allah. She would ask King Sulaiman.

When King Sulaiman heard she was coming, he was pleased and wanted to give her a sign that would show the power of Allah. So he decided to present her with her own throne.

King Sulaiman said to his courtiers, 'Who can bring me the Queen of Saba's throne before they come here on their knees?'

An *efreat*, a large and powerful jinn, said, 'I will bring it here to you before you even get up from this meeting. Really, I can do it and you can trust me.'

Another, who knew God's Truths, said, 'I'll bring it to you before an eye can blink.'

So it was done. The Queen's throne was brought.

When King Sulaiman saw how quickly the throne was standing in front of him, he said, 'This is how God works! Now this is a test for me to see whether I am thankful or ungrateful. Really, if anyone is grateful to God, it is good for him. If not, then remember that God is *al-Ghani* and *al-Kareem*—the highest in honour, glory and generosity.'

King Sulaiman said, 'Change the Queen's throne so that she won't be able to tell if it's hers or not. Let's see if God will guide her to the truth.'

King Sulaiman also commanded his builders, both jinn and men, to build a great pavilion with water flowing under a glass floor. He wanted to show the Queen that worshipping the sun was like believing that the glass floor was really water.

The Queen believes

The Queen of Saba and her people arrived. She told King Sulaiman, 'I have not come here proudly. Allah has guided me. We used to worship the sun, as you know. Now I have a new understanding. Now I believe in God.'

King Sulaiman was happy to hear this from the Queen of Saba. She was asked to come into the grand palace.

King Sulaiman presented the Queen of Saba with the throne. He asked her, 'Is this your throne?'

Surprised, she saw that it really was her throne and said, 'Yes. My throne was like this. I see that it was mine.'

As she walked towards the pavilion, the Queen saw the glass floor and thought it was flowing glistening water. She raised the hem of her skirts above the water. She was surprised when King Sulaiman told her, 'This is just a smooth palace floor. It's made of polished glass.'

Then the Queen understood. She said, 'Oh, I have made a mistake. I have been mistaken about everything. Things are not as they seemed to be.'

The Queen of Saba said, 'I do believe in Allah, and will worship Him, who is the God of the Worlds.'

King Sulaiman then helped her to learn more about Allah. She had come from a people who did not believe in Allah and so he taught her how to worship Allah.

This is how Allah taught his chosen prophets, Dawood and Sulaiman, some of His secrets. He told them to tell people to worship only one God and follow the path that leads to a happy end. They were both thankful for the knowledge and wisdom Allah had given them and said, 'Praise be to Allah, Who has favoured us above many of His servants who believe!' Allah says Dawood and Sulaiman both enjoy a beautiful place near to Him.

This story about King Dawood and King Sulaiman is found in the Noble Qur'an in several Surahs:

2:102,249-51	21:78-82,105	34:10-4
8:28	27:15-44	38:17-40

PROPHET ISA AND HIS MOTHER

(Peace Be Upon Them)

A special baby girl

For a long time after the Children of Israel had left Egypt with Prophet Musa, they lived in the land of Palestine. It was a land of hills and plains, with a deep river that flowed through it. It was a place where olives, figs, grapes and other fruits grew. There was plenty of green grass on the hills for their flocks of sheep and goats. The Children of Israel built many towns throughout the land.

In one of the towns there lived a noble family. They could trace their family back to Imran, the father of Musa and Haroon. They were faithful in their worship of Allah and always remembered how Allah guided the Children of Israel.

There was a woman in this family who was going to have a baby. She decided that she would devote her unborn child to Allah. She prayed, 'Oh my God! I make a promise to You. When my baby will be born, I will make sure that my child will grow up to do Your special work. You hear and know all things, so hear this from me.'

When the baby was born, she was surprised and said, 'Oh my God! My baby is a girl!'

Allah knew all about her child.

And she prayed to Allah, 'I have named her Maryam. I put her and her children in Your care. Protect them.'

In this family, there was a man on the right path named Zakariya. His wife was the cousin of Maryam, and he took charge of Maryam, to teach and guide her in learning about Allah.

As she grew up, Maryam spent more and more time alone, praying to Allah. Whenever Zakariya went into her room to see her, he found that somehow she had been given everything she needed. He said, 'Oh Maryam! Where does this come from?'

She said, 'From Allah. Allah gives whatever is needed to whoever He wishes, without limit.'

A messenger from Allah

Maryam grew up under Zakariya's special care. She learned to love Allah, and would go by herself, away from others to spend time praying. She put up a screen so no one could see her, and there she would be all alone for her prayers.

One day, an angel came to her. She thought it was a man and told him, 'If you believe in Allah, don't come. Don't bother me here.'

The angel said, 'No, I am only a messenger from your God, bringing you good news. Maryam, Allah has chosen you above the women of all the lands. Allah is sending you a gift. You will have a son.'

Maryam was very surprised. She said, 'Oh my God! How can I, all alone, have a son?'

The angel answered, 'Don't worry about it. Allah makes what He wills. When He has a plan, He just says to it 'Be' and it is. Oh Maryam, worship your God with a strong faith. This boy will be called Isa, the son of Maryam, and he will be of high rank in this world and the next. He will be among those who are nearest to Allah.'

The angel said more about Allah's gift to Maryam. 'Allah will teach the boy. He will be able to talk to people while he is still in the cradle, and he will grow up to be a wise man. Allah will make him a messenger to the Children of Israel.'

Maryam becomes a mother

So Maryam was going to have a baby. She went far away to a quiet place by herself for many days.

When she was hungry and thirsty, she prayed to Allah.

She heard a voice, 'Look down—your God has given you a stream of water. And look up—just shake the trunk of the palm tree and fresh dates will fall down to you. So eat and drink.'

Allah gave her whatever she needed.

In time, the baby was born.

Then Maryam went back to her people.

Maryam's son

When she brought the baby back to her people, carrying him in her arms, they said, 'Oh Maryam! This is really a surprise. Where did this baby come from?' But Maryam just pointed to the baby. They said, 'How can we talk to such a little baby?'

The baby answered, 'I am really a servant of Allah. He has showed me what is true and made me a prophet and is with me wherever I am. He has taught me to pray and to be good to others as long as I will live. He has asked me to be kind to my mother. So peace is with me all the time, the day I was born, the day that I die and the day that I shall be raised to life again.'

Maryam took good care of her very special son. His name was Isa.

The miracle

All children are born to their fathers and mothers. But Adam, the very first man, had no parents. Allah just made him from clay and put life in him and then he became a man. Then Allah made his wife and together they had children. And their children had children.

And Isa, the son of Maryam, was born without a father. Allah also made him in a very special way. He put a spirit in his mother's body and then Maryam gave birth to a child. This was a miracle. In this way, Allah made Maryam and her son Isa a sign for all people.

Right from the beginning, Isa was filled with wisdom from Allah. He had been talking to people while he was still in the cradle. Allah taught him the Book and the Torah, which other messengers had received from Allah. And Allah taught Isa a new book of good news called the Bible. The Bible was a message filled with light and guidance.

Maryam understood that her son was sent by Allah to be His messenger. She knew that whatever Isa said was true. She knew that whatever he showed her was Allah's will. And she knew that he had a very important message for the Children of Israel.

The word

Isa came with a message to the Children of Israel. 'I have come to you with wisdom, in order to clearly show you some of the things you doubt. You should fear God and listen to me. Allah is my God and your God. So worship Him. This is the straight way.'

Isa showed them many signs: 'I have come to you with a sign from your God. Look! I make the shape of a bird from clay, and then I breathe into it, and by Allah's will it becomes a real bird.'

'With the power of Allah, I cure blind people so that they can see again; I heal the lepers; I raise people who have died to life again—all by Allah's will.'

'I can tell you what you eat and what you store in your houses. There must be a sign for you in all this, if you only believe.'

Isa said, 'Oh Children of Israel! I am the messenger of Allah sent to you, to tell you that the Law which was sent before me is true. I will make part of what was forbidden to you before lawful for you now. And the good news is also true that a messenger named Ahmad will follow me.'

The followers

Some people believed in Isa and they became his disciples. Isa said, 'Who will be my helpers to do the work of Allah?'

The disciples said, 'We are Allah's helpers. We believe in Allah. You can see that we are people who follow Allah's will.'

And the disciples worked with Isa to teach the Children of Israel. Some of the people believed and some did not believe. For those who followed Isa, Allah filled their hearts with kindness. He guided them so that they could walk on the straight path, and He forgave the wrong things they had done in the past.

The disciples saw the miracles Isa did. He did these to give the people a sign that what he said was true. Then once, they asked for a special miracle for themselves.

They said, 'Oh Isa, the son of Maryam! Can your God send down to us a table set with food from heaven?'

Isa said, 'Fear Allah, if you have faith.'

They said, 'We only want to eat from there and satisfy our hearts, and know that you have really been telling us the truth. We ourselves want to see such a miracle.'

Then Isa the son of Maryam said, 'Oh Allah! Send to us from heaven a table set with food, so that there may be for us—the first and the last of us—a quiet festival and a sign from You. And provide for our strength, for You can best give us what we need.'

Allah said, 'I will send it down to you. But if any of you don't believe after that, I will punish him like no one else.'

So Allah gave the disciples the special miracle for which they had asked.

The disciples said, 'Our God! We believe in what you have showed us and we follow the messenger. So remember us as those who speak the Truth.'

The doubters

When some people saw that Isa could cure the lepers and the blind, raise the dead and could tell them what they had eaten in their homes, they said, 'Isa, the son of Maryam, is God.'

But Isa told them he was not God. 'Oh Children of Israel! Worship Allah, my God and your God.'

Many of the people were confused. Some of them, when they saw the miracles, said, 'This is magic!'

Then Allah said to Isa, 'Oh Isa! I will take you and raise you up to Myself and make you free of all the wrong things that people say about you. I will make your followers greater than the people who turn away from truth, on the day when the dead shall be raised to life again. Then everyone will return to me and I will judge everyone on the things on which they have disagreed. For the ones who turned away from truth, I will punish them with terrible pain in this world and in the next.'

The people who did not believe made many plots and many plans. Some of them planned to kill Isa by hanging him on a cross till he died.

But Allah had plans, too. He raised Isa up from this world to Himself.

After Isa was raised, some people said that they had crucified him. They boasted, 'We killed Isa, the son of Maryam, the messenger of Allah.'

'But they had not killed him. But that is how it appeared to them.

No, Allah raised him up to Himself. The best of planners was Allah.'

One day in the future

One day, Allah will gather all His messengers together and ask, 'What did people do when you gave them your message?'

They will say, 'We do not know. It is You who knows everything about all that is hidden.'

Then Allah will say, 'Oh Isa, the son of Maryam! Tell about my gifts to you and your mother.'

'Behold! I made you strong with my spirit, so that you spoke to the people when you were in the cradle and when you were old. Behold! I gave you wisdom. I taught you the Book, the Torah and the Bible. And behold! With My power, you made the shape of a bird out of clay and breathed into it and it became a bird. And with My power you healed the blind and the lepers. And with My power, you raised the dead. And behold! I did not let the Children of Israel harm you when you showed them the clear signs and those who did not believe said, 'This is nothing but magic.'

'And behold! I put a spirit among the disciples so that they would believe in Me and my messenger. They said, 'We have faith, and we bow to Allah as His followers.'

Then Allah will ask, 'Oh Isa, the son of Maryam! Did you tell people, "Worship me and my mother as gods?"'

And Isa will say, 'Glory to You! I could never say what I had no right to say. If I had said such a thing, You would have known it. You know what is in my heart, but I do not know what is in Yours. You know everything about all that is hidden. I never said anything to them except what You told me to say. It was: "Worship Allah, my God and your God." While I lived among them, I saw what they did. When You took me up, You saw what they did. You see everything. If You punish them, they are your servants. If You forgive them, You are the One with the power and wisdom.'

Allah will say, 'This is a day when the people who spoke the truth will be glad they were truthful. The home where they will live forever will be beautiful gardens, where rivers flow and they will be surrounded with everything they could want.'

Signs for all people

Isa, the son of Maryam, was sent in the footsteps of the other messengers. His uncle, Zakariya and his cousin, Yahya had come just before him. And before them were many other prophets. All of them had one and the same message: Believe and serve one God.

Isa had said, 'Oh Children of Israel! I am the messenger of Allah sent to you. I tell you that the Torah which was sent to you was true.' The Torah had been the Law of Allah given to Prophet Musa long ago. And Isa continued to tell his people, 'I have come to tell you the good news about a messenger who will come after me, whose name shall be Ahmad.'

Ahmad is the name for Prophet Muhammad (May the Peace and Blessings of Allah be upon Him), the last and greatest messenger from Allah who completed the long line of prophets. He completed Allah's message for people until the Day of Judgment. After him, no other prophet will come from Allah.

Allah's plan was that Isa should clearly show His signs to the Children of Israel. The people who believed became his followers, helping him to do the work of Allah. But many people were confused and many did not believe what he showed them and what he said. When he was born in such a miraculous way and was such a remarkable baby, many of them started to worship Isa and his mother Maryam. When he showed the people miracles, like healing the blind and the lepers, raising the dead and putting life into birds of clay, many said it was magic. They even made plans to crucify him. But Allah had another plan for Isa and raised him up to Himself.

In all these things, Allah made Maryam and her son, Isa, a sign for all people.

The story of Isa and his mother is found in the Noble Qur'an in different Surahs:

3:35-61	6:85	16:33	23:50	57:27
4:156-159,171	9:30,49	19:1-33	41:6	61:6,14
5:19,49,75-78,112-123	13:38	21:91	43:57-64	66:12.